FOOTSTEPS OF D-DAY

An easily read description of the 1944 D-Day invasion, and the Normandy of 1994, from a journalist who has spent a decade in research.

by

BRIAN WOODS

Published by Kent Publishing
APRIL 1994

Photographs:

June 1944

    US National Archives and Records Administration (Non-Textual Branch), Washington DC.

    The Imperial War Museum, London.

June 1988 to 1993

    Author, Corporate Visual Services, Al. Woods

NORMANDIE PUBLISHING

Email: corprel@senet.com.au

Tel: +618 8363 4494

Fax: +618 8363 5494

Post: PO Box 393, Kent Town 5071

South Australia AUSTRALIA

© Copyright Brian Woods
April 1994
All rights reserved

National Library of Australia
Woods, Brian
    Footsteps of D-Day
ISBN 0 646 18702 3

This book is copyright. Apart from any fair dealing for the purposes of private study, research, criticism or review, as permitted by the *Copyright Act 1968*, no part may be reproduced by any process whatsoever without the written permission of the publisher.

Wholly produced in Adelaide, South Australia
Graphics and Design: Harlen Graphics
Printing: Gillingham Printers Pty Ltd

CONTENTS

The Author vii

The Book ix

Acknowledgements xiii

CHAPTER ONE
Dunkirk to Normandy – A Prelude to D-Day 1

CHAPTER TWO
The Plan and the Forces 11

CHAPTER THREE
Assembly and Despatch 37

CHAPTER FOUR
Landings – Division of Territory 63

CHAPTER FIVE
The Towns 117

CHAPTER SIX
Principal Statistics 153

Line of Command 156

Notes to Photographs 157

Abbreviations 167

THE AUTHOR

Brian Woods is a journalist resident in Australia, who, during the past ten years, has researched the subject of D-Day from records held in archives in the United States, the United Kingdom, Australia, through interviews and in private collections. He has lived in, and covered the Normandy countryside, and as a photo journalist compiled a unique collection of comparative photographs, those featuring the Normandy of today being taken on, or close to the anniversary of D-Day each year.

He is the recipient of many advertising, art and film production awards, nationally and internationally, and his book is written in the advertising journalist's relaxed, communicative style.

THE BOOK

Extending from before even the early hours of the Day itself, the subject of D-Day has been thoroughly covered by many well informed and skilled writers. War correspondents, historians, the residents of Normandy, and the troops themselves from first hand knowledge, have contributed to the extensive amount of written and spoken material available.

With the passing of time, it is natural for there to be some conflict in accounts and for differing claims to emerge. Whether it was four Luftwaffe aircraft seen on the afternoon of the 6th of June, or two of them in the morning, or there were 35 sorties, (as separate documents claim), or the Crisbeq battery recorded two hits, or no hits, or whether the rail traffic was down 55% in May, (or 69%), could concern the purists, but for this book is of little material consequence.

Throughout, where significant doubt has been evident, the item has been investigated as thoroughly as it is possible to do, fifty years after the event, when some memories are no longer sharp, and untampered documentation sometimes difficult to track. In seeking to avoid inaccurate detail, there are footnotes where considered necessary, and on each occasion where a dead-end has been reached, the more conservative figure, or that which carries more weight of evidence has been recorded.

Most readers of this book's English version still relate to the Imperial measuring system, so primary measurements are given in Imperial form.

Similarly, trucks and lorries mean the same on opposite sides of the Atlantic, or the Pacific, so in the spirit of the D-Day joint venture, I have deliberately mixed these and other differing words to describe identical objects.

When many events are happening at one time, in a complex operation such as *Overlord*, code for the D-Day invasion, it is not possible to maintain continuity. Whilst preferring chronological order and a well arranged sequence, a text can become disjointed as it changes from event to event, one taking over the other, and that in turn being overtaken by yet another, the narrative frequently leaving and revisiting as each time frame passes. Where relativity is more important, I have chosen to continue with a single subject, even if it requires inclusion of events ahead of sequence.

Although D-Day information is readily available to the researcher from many sources, it is so involved, that inclusion of this weight of detail in a single volume would be both overwhelming and confusing for readers other than those committed to a study of military history.

My objective is to present a wide but clear picture of the lead-up, the planning, the Day, and the Normandy of the nineties, without any intention of attempting to match the intimate knowledge of those who were there, and whose experience no other person could hope, nor reasonably wish to emulate. For them, as for the others who survived, no matter on which side they fought, those memories and experiences are theirs, and should remain so.

In 1944, I was a child too young and too far away to know or be involved. The Japanese had been on our doorstep, and my country had been assaulted by that enemy many times. Although some of our servicemen and women were fighting in the European sector, our focus was on the Pacific. But it was the Normandy invasion, a battle in a remote country, which was the forerunner of the end of the war in Europe, permitting the flow-on release of resources into the Pacific, the swift end of Japanese resistance, and the end of World War Two.

Today, as an adult, even after many years visiting Normandy, I marvel at the intricate planning, the scale, and achievements, despite the adverse elements and relatively limited technology available. The ability of the defending German Army to hang on in the face of an assault mounted by an unrelenting enemy with seemingly inexhaustable supplies, is nothing short of astounding. With shortages of fuel and ammunition, their factories and supply lines under constant attack, their ground forces shot up by an enemy with almost total air superiority, and gross errors of judgement committed by their senior command, the German Army's performance in Normandy is one of the more remarkable events of the Second World War.

One cannot help but couple these thoughts with the knowledge that this was an invasion which could not afford to fail – an invasion, but for the exceptional deceptive skills of the Allies, the weight of their massive matériel and manpower, the errors of the defenders, and considerable good fortune, which nearly did.

Fifty years on, there is a different world, and a different Normandy from those years of Nazi occupation. Still the scene of the largest sea and air invasion in the history of mankind, the beaches are clean and peaceful. The refuse of war is gone, save for a rare piece of rusting metal occasionally uncovered by the Channel tides. Or the hulk which lies in the sea off *Utah Beach*, background for the trainers who exercise their horses on the hard, level sand, and the mussel farmers who tend their racks, supplying shellfish to the markets of France and other countries.

Normandy of the 1990s, is still the Normandy one imagines of centuries ago. Sunken lanes worn away by years of wheels and water, hedgerows and quietness, poppies and tall grass, the peace of an unspoiled countryside. A countryside marred only by the occasional concrete blockhouse and bunker, today overgrown with grass and brambles, which in a generation past, housed the defensive weapons of Hitler's Atlantic Wall, and the troops which manned the batteries.

Villages and towns, now restored, bear little evidence of war, but their people do not forget.

In market squares, the Tricolour and Stars & Stripes fly permanently side by side, streets and towns bear the names of generals, roadways are named after troops who fell, and beaches after the states of a foreign land thousands of miles away.

No, the French do not forget. Nor should we.

Adelaide, South Australia
April, 1994

ACKNOWLEDGEMENTS

Research involves poking in to every possible corner which may contain information, as well as the more conventional forms of information gathering. In a project of this length and complexity, the precise source of each piece of data, and the follow up check becomes blurred in the mass, as it just becomes one of those things that you know, but cannot recall how.

Obviously, books written by other authors provide considerable background, even if the content does not always agree, but the real value comes from people who themselves become involved and go to considerable lengths to help.

Cornelius Ryan's epic, *The Longest Day*, must be the benchmark for any study of D-Day, and with the film of the same name, provides an entertaining, informative background. Much of my earlier knowledge and interest comes from his work.

My thanks to Fred Pernell of the National Archives and Records Administration, Washington DC, and his friendly staff for their ready co-operation, and equally, to the Keeper of Photographs, Imperial War Museum, London, for the patience of his staff whilst I ferreted amongst the binders on their shelves during my many visits. Thanks also to the staff of the United States Consulate, Canberra, Australia for their guidance.

Other information comes from the London Daily Telegraph's reports, the BBC tapes recording bulletins from correspondents in Normandy, and from various sources in Normandy – Mayor Alexandre Renard's book *Sainte Mere Eglise*, leaflets, exhibits, signs, the excellent museums, even open air displays – the contact and correspondence with people who were there, and whose first hand knowledge was invaluable.

Special thanks to Harry Borysewicz of Harlen Graphics for his layouts and technical assistance and to Eric Sim of Gillingham Printers for his involvement.

Finally, my thanks to the people of Normandy, who accepted me, for whom nothing was too much trouble, and through whom I discovered many pieces of information not generally known. Especially M. & M. Eon, my friends at Ste Mere Eglise.

CHAPTER ONE

DUNKIRK TO NORMANDY
A PRELUDE TO D-DAY

It is probable no other event in history has been planned as carefully, with such precision, over as long a period, and amidst such deception and intrigue, as *Operation Overlord*, the invasion of France on the 6th of June 1944, known to history as D-Day.

Dunkirk, the defeat and near capture of the British Expeditionary Force, represented one of the lowest points in a long and terrible war. At the same time, the desperate rescue, completed on the 4th of June 1940, was a practical and public demonstration of the resourcefulness and grit which carried Britain through those years, and eventually, with their allies, back to the beaches of France four years almost to the day, afterwards.

There would be many returns before that massive official assault, the first of which was a defiant foray three weeks after Dunkirk, by a small party to the beaches south of Boulogne. This was little more than a seaborne version of the "rhubarbs" flown by allied fighter-bomber pilots later in the war, the intent being to stir up the enemy and inflict whatever damage was possible, with probably an element of defiance as well.

Later expeditions to the French coast had a far more significant purpose. Ferried by midget submarine, commando trained specialists systematically surveyed the Channel beaches, under the noses of German sentries, measuring inclines and distances, taking samples for analysis in Britain. The French Resistance, active throughout the country, was unable to obtain access to the beaches, so the only avenue for survey was from the sea.

Commandos came and went with regularity, completing their nocturnal assignments and usually avoiding capture. Generally, those who were captured, fell into the hands of the Gestapo and were subsequently shot, on a standing order issued by Hitler. A small raiding party of commandos landed in St Laurent sur Mer in September 1942, three of them being killed, and a survivor was subsequently captured and shot. Graves of the three can be seen in the town's church cemetery.

But the majority of intelligence gatherers returned with their information, however small, to form the montage which became *Operation Overlord*.

Two of these specialists, Major Logan Scott-Bowden and Sergeant Bruce Ogden Smith, successfully avoided land mines, automatic alarms, machine gun emplacements and sentries, crawling up these beaches, a probing knife testing ahead for mines, trailing behind a length of cord measured off at intervals so the area of each sample could be identified. They were key participants in what was an extensive and thorough programme of homework designed to reduce the odds of the invading forces being stuck on the beaches through natural or man made obstacles.

Their chance of capture was high, so many of the beaches they surveyed did not have the faintest chance of being the site of a future invasion. Their superiors knowingly sent them on many errands which were blinds, some, hundreds of miles away from the planned area. This was simple insurance against their being captured and divulging information under duress, information which if eventually extracted, would be so convoluted as to be completely useless to the enemy. Part of war's dirty tricks department of which there is more later.

Testing the beaches formed a vital part of the basic preparation for landing. Not much use unloading armour which will be bogged down the moment it lands and so become a sitting duck for artillery, clog the beaches and prevent the following troops and equipment from reaching solid ground.

Hit the beach and get off fast, is the principle for any amphibious operation, so the foundation has to be there, or vehicle design adapted to handle the conditions. This was the vital role performed by Scott-Bowden and Ogden Smith, their samples being analysed and matched with similar soil conditions in England. On English beaches, equipment was tested under identical conditions of traction and support. Some of it bogged, so designs were altered or landing sites changed.

Their response was often at the shortest of notice. Forty-eight hours before D-Day, a reconnaissance photograph indicated a patch of doubtful sand near Colleville sur Mer, soon to be known as *Bloody Omaha*. The two commandos were immediately despatched, and the following morning General Omar Bradley, commanding officer, US 1st Army ("The Big Red One"), received a jar of soil, cored that night from the beach under the muzzles of the German garrison.

Defences were examined and measured, metal samples hacksawed off and the damage concealed. The data obtained enabled full scale reproductions to be made to specification, and tested in conditions as close as possible to the actual situation. The effectiveness of tank defences was tested against actual equipment, the amount of explosive necessary to demolish obstacles established, and entire areas reproduced, complete with mines, flamethrowers, concrete emplacements and other defences upon which engineers could practice their hazardous occupation of mine and obstacle clearance.

Speed in clearing obstructions to a landing was necessary to reduce the period of exposure of the landing craft at sea. Craft packed with troops and equipment, slow moving, clearly in view, an artillery officer's dream, were vulnerable to a wide range of weaponry.

Swift, efficient and constantly moving, engineers who were to eventually suffer more than 50% casualties on the day, rehearsed their drill unceasingly on real life objects born of data captured from French beaches.

The methodology which was to be employed in the invasion was often the result of bitter and costly experience, and the Dieppe Raid is a prime example.

Throughout history, from Viking times to the adventures of privateers and operations of official navies, ports have been targeted for special attention. Apart from riches to be plundered, they provided the only facilities for a seaborne landing and access to the country, so consequently defences became increasingly sophisticated and effective. With the development of port defences came a rethink of assault methods, of which Drake's Cadiz raid represents the first relatively modern example.

Sea operations close to land were not unfamiliar to the newly appointed Director of Combined Operations, Vice-Admiral Lord Louis Mountbatten. An imaginative and daring tactician, designer of the Navy's then modern signalling systems, veteran of spectacular destroyer flotilla operations as commanding officer of the Fifth Destroyer Flotilla, Mountbatten was a legend. His destroyer, HMS *Kelly*, in May 1940, survived a torpedo attack, and decks awash, barely made it to the Tyne, by coincidence the shipyard of her builders. A year later, *Kelly* was dive bombed and sunk off Crete, and her commanding officer returned home to take up his new post.

In the spring of 1942, it was recognised that St Nazaire, where the liner *Normandie* was built in a specially constructed dock, was the only port on the Atlantic coast with facilities capable of handling service and repairs to the six German battleships cooped up in Brest and Norway, should they break out to ravage shipping in the Atlantic. Particularly, the graving dock at St Nazaire was the object of the Allies' attention, and a raid was planned under Lord Mountbatten's direction, in which it was intended to run an explosive packed destroyer into the dock gates, scuttle her and leave time delay fuses to complete the work.

The lend lease destroyer, *Campbelltown*, built in 1919, was selected as the modern day fireship to be supported by a mixed eighteen-vessel flotilla of motor torpedo boats, a motor launch and motor gunboat carrying a force of 277 commandos in addition to their crews – a total of 630 officers and men. The *Normandie* dock was well inside the harbour, and although the assault fleet ran a gauntlet of heavy fire, suffering severe losses, *Campbelltown* smashed into the dock gates at eighteen knots, and at noon the next day blew up, followed many hours later by two torpedoes, fired during the raid, which had lain on the harbour floor. The dock remained useless for the remainder of the war.

Encouraged, another raid was organised, this time with the intent of landing and inflicting as much damage as possible. Shadowing the obvious was a deeper purpose, a pilot test to gauge the practicality of invasion through a harbour. The port selected – Dieppe.

The date – August 19th, 1942.

The Dieppe operation itself was by all apparent measures, a disaster. A disaster so bad, that records were not released for thirty years. Of more than 6,000 men, 4,300 became casualties, 3,360 of them Canadians. Amongst a total of 28 Churchill tanks engaged, only fifteen reached the foreshore, and of them, a scant three managed to make it into town and their swift destruction. Apart from the fact that the Germans knew of the raid beforehand, it became obvious that frontal attack against a well defended port was destined for failure, and to this extent the Dieppe raid was a success. It gave the Allies a clear direction for the planning of what was to become known as *Operation Overlord*, the invasion of France.

As clear as it was to the Allies, the Germans formed the opposite opinion. For Hitler, Dieppe was the forerunner of many more harbour defeats of invading forces, and confirmation of his long held opinion that the main landing would be through a port. The generals told him, "as long as we hold the ports, we hold Europe." His conviction, and that of Field Marshal Gerd von Rundstedt, was Pas-de-Calais. It was logical.

Short crossing, close and constant air support, even the capacity to lob shells from long range guns. Tight, better guarded lines of communication, swift replenishment of matériel, fuel and troops made Pas-de-Calais the overwhelming choice.

From then, it could be said, for Germany, the coming invasion was lost.

Dieppe taught the Allies that extensive neutralising of defences, supplies, and supply routes was vital, they learned a bitter security lesson, and the necessity for skilful and extensive deception. The importance of planning in minute detail, with selection and testing of equipment under identical conditions was vividly underscored. "If a port cannot be captured we must take one with us" said Mountbatten. And the Allies did. In many areas, Dieppe was the foundation stone for *Overlord*.

From this time, there occurred a programme of deception and duplicity, involving the sacrifice of hundreds of lives in the interests of saving thousands later. A game of deception unequalled in scale or ingenuity. And it was played on both sides, with Germany striving to discover the place of an invasion attempt, and the Allies striving to conceal and deceive.

Espionage in Britain, through import of German agents, appeared to be plagued by disaster, however well planned or imaginative each foray may have been. Some of course, were not well planned at all, with inaccurate and scanty briefing. Throughout, a total inadequacy in understanding British custom and psyche haunted them, producing basic errors such as asking a publican for an early morning drink when everyone but the spy knew that pubs did not open until 10.30 am. Or offering food coupons at a restaurant when restaurants did not require them.

Espionage agents stumbled into the country via beaches already occupied by troops, others broke limbs on landing. Some, entering by more conventional means, were subjected, with their belongings, to a long and exhaustive search, a search by experienced and perceptive investigators. Investigators who knew that pyramidon powder made invisible ink, that manufacturers' tags on garments did not correspond with the actual clothing the manufacturer produced, or simple mix-ups by their quarry who could not get to grips with a non-decimal currency system.

There were spies who were equipped with elaborate documents as cover, but which actually caused their downfall. Joseph Vanhove, a Belgian, caught by the Gestapo collaborating with a German officer running a black market operation, was given the choice of death or work as a spy. His logical choice found him in England with a fistful of forged newspaper clippings from Belgian newspapers published by the Germans, describing his Resistance activities, and placing him on a most-wanted list. His escape to Britain was through enemy occupied territory, with informers and the Gestapo breathing down his neck.

Vanhove, arrested and tried in May 1944, was hanged in July, simply because it did not occur to him that nobody in their right mind would escape through occupied Europe, carrying a wad of papers which would instantly incriminate them if questioned and searched.

Some spies were "doubled"[1], and for a time were useful. Almost without exception, the majority of those caught were hanged. A very few avoided capture, and some, when detected, were placed under surveillance, and used without their being aware. After all, apart from aerial reconnaissance, how else could word of the buildup at Dover be arranged to reach the enemy?

Outside Britain, in neutral countries, or those professing to be neutral,

---

1 Doubling is a procedure used by both sides where a captured agent is put to work as though still free, sending misleading information home, the alternative being a rope or firing squad.

espionage thrived, with the two sides watching, each knowing who the other was, circling in an atmosphere of impotent standoff, but there were exceptions. *Cicero*, for instance.

Cicero, Elyesa Bazna, was valet to the British Ambassador in Ankara, Sir Hughe Knatchbull-Hugessen, and over a period of six months, Bazna had systematically photographed documents passing through the embassy safe. He had the potential to be the most damaging spy in the German network, but so reliable was he, and so detailed the information provided, that his masters doubted its accuracy. Minutes of Allied conferences, passing through the embassy, were carefully photographed and the film sent to Berlin. The news they contained was bad news for Germany, and the Führer did not welcome bad news. Bad news was dismissed and the bearers placed in peril, so bad news was best buried.

The documents contained news of a war already won by the Allies, and their post war plans. They told of a massive American industrial machine pouring quantities of war matériel into Britain, Italy and the Russian front. The Germans read of plans for their own post war fate, which delighted them less, so of course the documents containing this bad news had to be forgeries. They also read of an operation code named *Overlord*, but this was accorded much the same treatment as other intelligence. Eventually *Cicero's* activities were discovered by Britain, security improved, Bazna escaped with the forged money with which he had been paid by the Germans, and the flow of information ceased.

Nevertheless, the word was exposed. *Overlord*.

What it meant was not known, but the suspicion formed that it was code for a large seaborne landing and this aroused the curiosity of Brigadenführer Walther Schellenberg, chief of SS Intelligence. Schellenberg's deadly tussle with Admiral Canaris, head of the Abwehr, now placed him, in April 1944, in the position of having to discover time and place of the invasion. And for Germany, time was running out.

Resistance organisations in occupied countries provided vital intelligence. A map, ten feet in length, and three wide, stolen from the Organisation Todt HQ in Caen and smuggled to England, detailed defence emplacements from Honfleur to Cherbourg – details which were not changed because nobody had the courage to report the loss.

Scraps of information on all subjects from the troops' diet to regimental deployment, were pieced together with other data, to form an intricate picture, as thousands of patriots worked to eject the occupiers of their countries, conveying information to the Allies for assistance in the assault they were to launch. Many sacrificed their own lives to save thousands of other lives on beaches, and throughout the countryside.

In the closing days of the Cherbourg resistance, Major Friedrich Küppers, when visited in his massive Osteck fortification by a delegation headed by US Major General Barton under a flag of truce, was dumbfounded when shown the map of his own fortifications, a map more detailed than his own, even to the billets, the numbers and units of troops throughout the area. There was only one error; Lieutenant Ralf Neste had been killed on the 5th of May in a Panzerfaust accident, but his name was still on the map. The shattered Küppers surrendered.

In the department of dirty tricks, the Allies excelled. *Operation Holland*, the parachuting of many well misinformed spies in to Holland, where they were captured and interrogated, divulging supposed secrets of an intended landing in Holland, and other items which were also inaccurate, contributed to the misleading of the enemy. All but three of these spies were executed. One of the survivors, a Dutchman, Hubert Lauwers, spent a frustrating period as a double, deliberately failing to give his correct security code in transmissions, so the Allies would suspect all was not well, cleverly conveying, in his messages, indications of the German trap so no more espionage agents would be sent. But still they came. At one stage, London even reminded him of the security code error! The truth of the operation may never be known, as all records were fortuitously burnt at the end of the War.

Frederic Donet, a French Sergeant, tough and pragmatic, joined the Mithridate section of the Resistance on the fall of France, and as a senior operator, codenamed *Lafleche*, was much wanted by the Gestapo. Donet was given a sophisticated transmitter from which to broadcast intelligence from Pas-de-Calais on the presumption that Calais would be the place of landing.

The transmitter, he was assured, was not traceable by existing German detection equipment, and so it was, that during a lengthy and comfortable session, the door burst open and his room filled with German troops. There is no question Donet was set up.

Simply, the wavelength was that used by German tanks in Calais. English intelligence knew this, because amongst many other eavesdropping activities, they monitored the tanks' transmissions. Capture, red-handed, of a senior Resistance officer, actively at work in Pas-de-Calais, was for the Germans, further confirmation that a landing would be in the area. Sentenced to death, Donet was rescued by the Belgian Resistance.

Assembling the weight of evidence of this, and a comprehensive list of betrayals of Resistance or Allied espionage agents, under code names *Holland, Fortitude, Starkey* or *North Pole*, there is little doubt that many lives were purposely sacrificed in this mini war within a war. Here was a war of deception with but a single objective, that of concealing the planned landing site, and ensuring the concentration of German defences as far from that site as possible.

So Pas-de-Calais it had to be, although this was not completely set in the defenders' minds. German intelligence, touchy and confused, named successively, La Rochelle, Belgium, Pas-de-Calais, the Seine estuary at Le Havre, Marseilles, Bordeaux and Brittany as possible invasion objectives.

But constantly, when logic prevailed, Pas-de-Calais was their choice.

CHAPTER TWO

THE PLAN

AND THE FORCES

The answer to the question, *Why was invasion day named D-Day?*, is that despite some plausible tales as to the origin, there is no convincing reason for this now descriptive part of everyday language. As with the naming of the operation itself, *Overlord*, or even any of the many other operations, the sometimes exotic titles for which can be the product of individual inventiveness, D-Day has no particular reason for its label. It seems this could just as easily have been X-Day.

Choices

And, for choice of landing, when Calais, or Holland, or South of France, or even Brittany were available – Why Normandy?

An important consideration favouring Normandy, as with any project of deception, is that it was one of the least expected. From an Allied viewpoint, much of Von Runstedt's dogma fitting his belief in Calais, did make Calais the most practical military choice.

Short crossing, minimum exposure during the journey, easy to replenish and support, easiest to defend, with aircraft endurance over target being longer, and shorter journey home to refuel, tighter communications, and with an estimated five days to the Rhine, geographically closer to Germany's jugular – the heartland of German war production.

Traditionally, invading armies have made the capital their objective, and Calais was also closest to Berlin.

But in two important aspects, Calais failed.

One, it was a port. The Allies knew from bitter experience that attempting to capture ports was bad news, and they also knew that if they did capture one, the resultant devastation of assault and destruction by the retreating army would make it unusable for weeks, possibly months.

No, it could not be a port.

Two, an invasion through Calais was expected. The area was a fortress, with the largest concentration of troops, very heavily defended, and any attempt to invade through the port would be expensive at best. Apart from this, although the short route to German production centres was an attraction, their close proximity also represented an advantage for the defenders in terms of supply. Settling the matter was the fact that the area around Dover could not accommodate the initial volume required for an invasion. So Calais was not a practical option, and neither was despatch through Dover.

The terrain of Holland was unsuitable for amphibious landings, and distance for fighter protection was a problem. Similarly, Brittany was too far to travel without detection and attack. Air protection was at its limit, the ports in the area were well defended, and apart from the ports, which we know were not an option, suitable landing sites were well separated.

Normandy also, was a considerable distance from Britain, and that was a drawback, but to balance this, the Germans thought so too, which assisted with the programme of deception. As with Holland and Brittany, but not as critical, effective time over target for support aircraft was reduced in comparison with Calais, and turnaround time longer. On a coastline unprotected from the northern weather, which could be nasty, the beaches were open, wide and exposed to gunfire. The tides covered a considerable amount of sand, so operations were subject to tidal movement, and it was just about the furthest point from the Rhine, a distance which would have to be fought bitterly all the way.

In favour was the relatively light defence system. The emphasis of course is on relatively, because Normandy was still well defended, and under the influence of Field Marshal Erwin Rommel, becoming increasingly more so. Compensating the long distance required for the advance, was the distance the Germans had to cover to support their army, and the vulnerability of supply lines.

Despite being open, the nature of the beaches favoured a seaborne landing, and whilst not as close as Dover for air support, 40% of the airfields in Britain were still within half an hour's flying time. Although at the limit, laying a fuel pipeline to Normandy was practical, and the sea crossing could be made by the invasion fleet in one period of darkness. Provided the handicaps of weather and lack of harbour facilities were overcome, Normandy remained the best option.

The active invasion section of *Overlord* was planned to form two stages. The landing and consolidation by occupation of coastline and key towns, then the move inland, supported by established supply lines channelled through an expanded network of ports and facilities. The first stage was *D-Day*, the second, the *Battle of Normandy*.

Under the Supreme Commander, (General Dwight D. Eisenhower), and Deputy Supreme Commander (Air Chief Marshal Sir Arthur Tedder), the assault forces were primarily divided into the three mediums of Sea, Air and Land, with Naval operations commanded by Admiral Sir Bertram Ramsay, Air operations by Air Chief Marshal Sir Trafford Leigh-Mallory, and Army (21st Army Group) by General Sir Bernard Montgomery. Reporting to General Montgomery were Lt Gen Omar Bradley, commander of the US 1st Army, and Lt Gen M. C. Dempsey, commander of the 2nd British Army.

Naval operations were simarly divided, with US forces supporting the US Army, and British forces supporting the British and Canadian troops. The Western Task force (US) covering the *Utah* and *Omaha* sectors

(St Vaast, east to Ste Honorine/Port en Bessin) was under the command of Rear Admiral Alan Kirk, USN, and the Eastern Task force, covering Port en Bessin, east to Ouistreham, was commanded by Rear Admiral Sir Philip Vian, RN. The Western Force comprised Forces U and O, with backup Force B, and the Eastern consisted of Forces G, J and S, backed by Force L.

In the air, under the leadership of Air Chief Marshal Leigh-Mallory, were the 9th US Air Force commanded by Lt Gen Lewis Brereton USAF, and 2nd Tactical Air Force commanded by, Air Marshal Sir Arthur Coningham, RAF.

Defences
Germany occupied 10,000 miles (16,000 km) of coastline, and spread along the coast of Northern France were emplacements housing an astounding array of armaments, from field and naval guns to the notorious German "88s". This cocktail of assembled variations totalled more than 90 different types, covering more than 25 calibres, using more than 250 varieties of ammunition, 20% of which was no longer available, and came from no less than ten countries. They were served by an equally varied collection of vehicles – German, French, Italian, Belgian, Polish, Russian, even British.

The emplacements, usually constructed by men and women of Reichminister Albert Speer's slave labour Organisation Todt, varied in quality, according to their haste of construction and the ability of the workers to sabotage concrete quality. They ranged from massive reinforced casements, which today, as photographs show, are still virtually indestructible, some having taken enormous punishment. Others were hurriedly constructed of concrete building blocks reinforced with steel rods, and tended to fall apart under bombardment.

The large defence complexes were interconnected with open trenches or covered tunnels. Until recently, the Crisbeq battery was one of the best examples of concrete trench construction. Linked by open passages more than 12 feet (3.7 metres) deep, the bramble overgrown channels presented a danger to unwary tourists or wandering cattle, and from 1990, most have been covered with earth.

In style of defence, Rommel and Von Runstedt differed completely. Rommel advocated heavy resistance at the beachfront to cause the enemy to falter and fail to establish a toe hold. Then, with fresh, unharmed reserves brought up from the rear, to punch home an attack from behind, move through the forward defences which had borne the initial impact of the incoming assault, and push the invaders back into the sea. Von Runstedt favoured beachfront defences to slow and weaken the enemy, infantry and light artillery to harass and further weaken as they proceeded inland, and as the third stage, heavy artillery, seasoned units, and armour to complete the job.

The German fortifications, controlled by units of the 7th Army, varied from clifftop emplacements to isolated concrete defences sited in the middle of fields behind the sandhills. Along these hills, often spaced well apart, the guns commanded a field of fire which would sweep the beaches. Behind, as in the case of Crisbeq and Azeville, they were in some instances 3 or 4 miles (5-6.5 km) from the beach, designed to combat shipping well out to sea, and avoid the initial beach assault.

Along the coast, the principal heavy emplacements were sited at Morsalines, Quineville, Ozeville, Azeville, Crisbeq (St Marcouf), and manned by the 709th and 91st German Infantry Divisions. Grandcamp Maisy, Pointe du Hoc, Longues sur Mer, Arromanches, Colleville sur Orne, Riva Bella, Ouistreham were the responsibility of the 716th Division, and Merville the 711th Division under the 15th Army.

Between these major fortifications were numerous smaller emplacements housing a variety of weapons, from heavy calibres down to machine guns which operated from concrete foxholes built into the side of the sandhills and entered through a small rear aperture. With very few exceptions, all were directed seawards, and not capable of effectively combating a land approach from the rear.

Within each defensive pod were dormitories, eating areas, communication rooms, storage, and workshop facilities, as well as the gunrooms. In total, the defences comprised an estimated 60 divisions, with support from Panzer Group West, the administrative arm of all tank divisions in northern France.

Between Arromanches and Ouistreham were grids of stiffened steel mesh, submerged upright, laced with mines and jagged at the top, ready to rip or blow the bottom out of any craft passing overhead. Each measuring about 10 feet square, *Element C*, as the obstructions were labelled, was designed for effectiveness at low tide, backing up the shallow water and hard sand defences. It created a particularly hazardous situation, as frogmen had to work underwater in murky conditions, where error could explode one or more of the mines. *Element C* could not be removed by setting one demolition charge, and each section had to be cleared piece by piece.

On the beaches, apart from the railway irons, and their mines, were wire entanglements, concrete obstacles, and supplementing them, *Rommel's candles* – mines mounted on poles angled out to sea. Submerged at high tide, they were designed to blow the bottom out of any craft impacting them on the way to the shore, and did.

Inland from the beaches, fixed fortifications were rare, with the emphasis being upon mobile units stationed in villages and towns – Grenadier regiments, Flak and Panzer (tank) units provided artillery, infantry, anti-aircraft and armoured defence, as well as assault capabilities.

So from the shallows where mines on poles were set to blow the bottoms out of vessels approaching at high tide, an army heading inland or landing from the air would have to avoid or overcome railway iron triangles with mines designed to prevent landing of both small vessels and amphibious vehicles, concrete fortifications housing an assortment of weapons from heavy naval, to machine guns, tackle sandhills liberally sown with mines, take their chances with the wires and stakes in fields installed as a deterrent for airborne landings, then fight the mobile forces.

This combination presented a formidable opposition to any invader, but in addition, fields and low lying country, particularly the Dives Valley, had been flooded. The inundated areas were to claim the lives of many paratroopers, who, dropped from an aircraft off course, and weighted down with a heavy pack and equipment, sank into the water and drowned.

It is astounding, that even though a landing in the area was not fully expected, the resources of an embattled Germany, fighting or threatened on at least four fronts, could still muster what by any measure was an awesome defence of what was not yet a battle zone, and in the opinion of most, never would be.

Tackling the defences

Merville, a battery close to the Orne, but on the Le Havre side, presented a particular problem.

Occupied by more than 150 men of the 1716th Artillery Regiment, it contained, according to intelligence, four or five 150mm long range guns, aimed along the coast, past Ouistreham, Luc sur Mer, Riva Bella, and right across the British sector beaches. The havoc this emplacement would cause did not require much imagination, and a plan was drawn up for Merville to be a priority target for capture and destruction. Adding to the Allies' conviction that Merville was a formidable object, was the massive concrete protection and elaborate network of defences surrounding the guns.

Apart from the concrete fortifications and the expected heavy guns, were 22 machine gun emplacements, some of which were 20mm AA. In front were barbed wire obstacles, leading to a minefield 110 yards (100 metres) wide. Behind that was a field of barbed wire 15 feet (4.5 metres) deep, and 5 feet high, and leading to the complex, the ground was covered with trenches, trip wires, with mines salted throughout. The entire layout was surrounded with a livestock fence. Merville's weakness was in its people, a garrison augmented with Russian conscripts and others. Given the option of fighting for Germany or extermination, their choice was obvious, but confronted with a determined invader, it was more likely they would hoist a white flag than provide resistance.

In a corner of England, near Newbury, an exact replica of Merville was built, duplicating the real battery, even to the livestock outside the perimeter. Every day for two months, under the command of twenty-nine year old Lt Col Terence Otway, the 750 troops who were to assault the fortifications, practised constantly. Using an elaborate assortment of equipment, from purpose made explosives to flamethrowers, bangalore torpedoes, and even amplifiers, they planned and rehearsed tactics repeatedly, for there was no question that the emplacement had to be taken before the first of the escort and landing vessels came within range. Merville was seen to be the principal threat to the British-Canadian sector landing, and the force which had the responsibility of neutralising it held no illusions as to their chances of survival.

Benouville bridge, spanning the Orne, and principal target for Major John Howard's group from the 6th British Airborne Division, was another vital objective. It was essential that it be captured intact, but intelligence indicated that it was both well defended and wired for demolition. The assault had to be swift and positive, and a pitched battle with the defenders avoided, as it would create a delay, and give them time to destroy the bridge. So a detailed replica was built, and stopwatch – timed practice occupied Howard's men for most of the Spring.

Fortune smiled

Rehearsals for anything can be a problem, concerts, weddings, plays, parades, even invasions. People arrive late or not at all, forget their places, muff their lines, and generally don't take the event seriously. But war rehearsals can be deadly, as commanders of the force practising an assault on one British beach discovered. In the participating assault craft were officers entrusted with the plans of the D-Day operation. They had to be, as they were part of the landing, and key officers had to know what was planned, so they could run their divisions as part of that plan. Those officers were codenamed *Bigots*.

A *Bigot* was one of more than a hundred Allied officers entrusted with the date and place of the invasion, the targets of each section of the forces, and were a prime potential source of accidental leak. As *Bigots* were to form an active part for the D-Day invasion force, they participated in training for the landings, according to their unit and place in the programme.

Apart from the *Bigots*, the participating troops in this exercise did not know the name of the beach they were to assault, nor even the code name. However, fortifications and defences had been faithfully duplicated, bombers laid a live carpet at a safe distance ahead of the troops, and without the gunfire, this was to be the closest to the real thing as it could be. Watched by the Allied command, *Exercise Tiger*, a rehearsal by Force U for the *Utah Beach* landing, took place on Slapton Sands in late April.

It was a disaster.

Not only did it run well behind schedule, and appear to be treated as a picnic by the participants, but unknown to General Eisenhower, who was not informed until the evening afterwards, a number of the landing craft en route to the beach at night had been attacked by German E Boats off Lyme Regis, and several hundred troops killed. Searchlights on, the enemy torpedo boats passed amongst the survivors, and if one of the *Bigots* happened to be amongst those rescued, the D-Day plan was in danger of becoming known.

Missing were ten *Bigots*. Drowned, or rescued by the enemy, nobody knew, so a massive operation of body retrieval was mounted. The Channel waters were desperately combed for the missing, and although at the end of the operation, hundreds of ordinary troops still remained unaccounted for, the ten specials, the *Bigots*, were claimed from the sea. The *Overlord* secrets were still safe, and Germany did not know how close a flotilla of prowling E boats came to uncovering the details so desperately sought.

The beaches

The Invasion Beaches stretch from St Vaast in the West, through Quinneville, to Grandcamp Maisy, Pointe du Hoc, Colleville sur Mer, and Ste Honorine, to Port en Bessin, Ouistreham and Benouville, a distance of approximately 56 miles (90 km). They were divided into *Utah*, and *Omaha*, (USA and France), and from Port en Bessin onwards were code named *Gold*, *Juno* and *Sword*, being the British, Canadian and French commando sectors. These names are applied to the beaches today.

At low tide, particularly in the *Utah* area, which exposes approximately 300 yards (275 metres) of sand, the beaches are flat and mostly firm. There are a few rocky headlands and some cliffs, but mostly fine clean sand leading up from the shallows to rows of low tussocky sand-hills, behind which are villages, fertile Norman farms, low set lanes, hedgerows, and the divided fields so typical of Bocage country.

There are rare patches of beach which are not quite as firm as the surrounds, and even walking on them can cause a person to slip or bog down in clay or dark silt. The soil samples brought back to Britain by Scott-Bowden and Ogden Smith, and from their later foray to *Omaha* for a check sample, enabled soil experts to identify the potential problems, but not provide the imaginative solutions necessary.

Hobart's Funnies – and others

Major General Sir Percy Hobart could perhaps have been considered an eccentric or an inventive genius, but either way, his talent for providing solutions was well recognised. In charge of an experimental armoured division, Hobart's talents were engaged by General Brooke, to overcome the problems of armour sinking into the sand, or being disabled by mines. He was requested to design armour for clearing obstacles, armour to provide a platform, and armour to swim.

From the fertile minds of Hobart and his team came a series of weird contraptions which worked. There was the Bobbin tank, a normal vehicle with a huge roll of material suspended in front, from which it could lay its own matting track over the patches of dubious beach which had been identified by previous surveys. The Flail or Crab tanks carried chains attached to central rotating axles, the ends of each chain flogging the mined sand in front, detonating explosives and clearing a path for the following equipment and infantry. An alternative was the Bangalore tank which fired the Bangalore torpedo, more usually employed for clearing wire and concrete barriers, but this time used to explode mines in front of the vehicle, and clear a path through minefields. Turretless tanks were designed to move up the beach and snug in against the seawall, forming a ramp for the other armour to climb over, and the Crocodile flamethrowing tanks were designed to clear concrete defences of their inhabitants. There was also the bridge laying AVRE – Armoured Vehicle, Royal Engineers.

But the amphibious tank, the tank that swam, was vital to the armoured invasion. Labelled the DD (Duplex Drive), the original adaptions of Valentine tanks were of Hungarian design, but with serious faults in flotation capacity and steering. Hobart seized these prototypes and successfully applied the principle to the American Sherman, around which a flotation skirt was fitted and other modifications installed, most in the United States at time of manufacture. In addition to Hobart's inventions were others, devised for similar purposes, and attached to a variety of vehicles. As a mine exploder, *Hedgerow*, an assembly of projectiles fired from landing craft, succeeded in exploding land mines through the concussion of their explosions.

Personal equipment for the troops was designed for a range of tasks, from preserving the body warmth of frogmen, to minimising the effect of underwater explosions. From a series of experiments in Portsmouth during which frogmen were subjected to underwater blasts of different intensity, a special protective kapok suit and jacket was swiftly developed to reduce the consequences of explosions during mine clearing operations in the initial landing phase.

With the passing of time, came an increased likelihood that the operational plan would be discovered by Germany, either through a piece of chance information falling into place, or through an accidental event of appalling misfortune.

Sensitive to any alterations to the deployment of troops, or any movement whatever in Northern France, planners became increasingly nervous as the date approached. Preservation of the twin secrets – date and place, but more important, the latter, was uppermost in the minds of the planners. Military exercises in southwest England, ports rapidly filling up with shipping, streets, laneways and country roads lined with vehicles, because there was nowhere else to park them, made deception extraordinarily difficult.

An island crammed full of servicemen, servicewomen and supplies, with airfields criss-crossing fields, ports packed with shipping, invited curiosity, or even some guesswork. Whole sections of the countryside were cut off from civilian entry, or taken over for rehearsals, and training on beaches with live ammunition provided a realism as close to battle conditions as possible. The entire southern part of England was a huge bivouac and storage depot where troops camped under canvas.

Trucks, armour, and other vehicles camouflaged to blend with hedgerows, lined laneways and village streets. With parachutists on practice drops descending out of the night upon peaceful villages and frightening the population, rangers scaling cliffs and armoured vehicles churning sands once thronged with holidaymakers, it seemed nigh impossible for an operation of this size to build up undetected by the enemy. Surely someone would wake up and piece the jigsaw together.

Narrow squeaks

But nobody did, at least nobody with a serious intent to betray the plan, although three schoolboys came close. Attending a school where the senior master was also one of the composers of the *Daily Telegraph* crossword, the trio was given crossword designs to complete as punishment – an alternative to the customary "lines".

One of the boys, also a member of the local cadets, had freedom of a nearby US army camp, where he regularly noticed and read maps, plans, and even managed to obtain photographs. In isolation, the information may not have meant much, but assembled in the perceptive teenager's mind, the accumulation revealed a massive operation, the layout of which he translated into a map on his bedroom wall.

Accurately, the schoolboy identified Normandy, code named the beaches, even listed the code for the massive caissons which were to form the artificial harbours. Gradually, correctly marked areas came to take shape in a village teenager's bedroom, and immersed as he was in his research, the words he had absorbed were those which came most naturally to mind during the task of composing his crossword punishment.

On May 2nd, the crossword clue for 17 across was *Utah*. On May 22nd, 3 down; *Omaha*. May 27th, 11 across; *Mulberry* (code for the caissons), and May 30th, the king-hit, *Overlord*, also 11 across. This was followed by the clue *Britannia and he hold the same thing*, with the answer *Neptune*, being code for *Overlord's* naval operations. The flap this created in Whitehall can be imagined, and a quiet interview of the official crossword composer occurred, without action being taken, or it appears, without the boys' involvement emerging until later.

And then there was the day the window blew open. One windy morning in May, a gust blew through the corridors of the War Office in London, carrying with it a number of copies of *Overlord* through a window and out into the street. All but one was recovered, and that had been handed by a pedestrian to a policeman further down the road.

One forgetful person left the complete portfolio of *Overlord* in a train, a garrulous party-goer said more than intended, and one particular son, who confided in mother and father, placed thousands of lives, and possibly the operation itself, in peril.

Boasting at a party, that life would improve for Londoners from June, caused the demotion and transfer home of one US General, and for one British officer, arrest, after he had told his parents the date – an indiscretion reported by the father.

A package arrived in a Chicago post office. Badly wrapped, the contents spilled out and were examined by postal employees who noticed in detail, a plan to invade Normandy beaches, a plan of the areas and the date, as well as the forces allocated to each section. The sender, a tired sergeant working in Allied Command, had mixed his parcels. Instead of papers being forwarded to Army Transportation in Washington, and a gift to his sister, the serviceman accidentally mixed the addresses. So Washington received the gift, and the vital documents landed on the Chicago mailroom floor.

In this atmosphere of crossword clues, scattered documents, careless chatter of a few, and a succession of incredible errors, the largest sea, air and land operation the globe had ever experienced was being planned. Although there were some on the German side who even believed an invasion would not occur, the enemy was still ignorant of the two vital factors – where and when. The south of England was sealed, and elaborate steps were taken to keep the enemy's expectation of Pas-de-Calais alive.

Deceit

Fortitude, code name for one of the largest operations of deception of the war, was created to develop this expectation to the full. In Dover harbour, were masses of small vessels in and around the area, lines of tanks, with obvious tracks running across the landscape, lines of lorries and aircraft. These were mostly plywood cutouts, or inflated rubber imitations, which changed around under cover of darkness, and were poorly camouflaged, so reconnaissance photographs could clearly identify the buildup of equipment.

The almost non-existent fighter defences and the inaccurate anti-aircraft fire did not seem unusual to the occasional German pilot brave enough to run the gauntlet and photograph the scene below. Tracked by Allied radar almost from the time of takeoff, these occasional enemy reconnaissance flights enjoyed protected bird status, for it was most important their film reached Berlin. As an important part of the deception process, troops were camped in Sussex and Kent, and this was further confirmation to German Intelligence that the invasion, if it came, would be from the Dover coastal region, and Pas-de-Calais was closest.

Adding to the buildup of deception, was the rule that for every bomb dropped on Normandy, two must be dropped in the Bolougne, Pas-de-Calais area, a procedure which was followed up to, and including the eve of D-Day. Commander of the 21st Army Group, General Sir Bernard Montgomery, worked in Portsmouth. Now, if the invasion was to be conducted from Dover, logically he would have been there, not Portsmouth, so steps were taken to make sure the enemy knew beyond doubt that he was in Dover. A dummy headquarters was created in Kent, to which all his radio messages were directed, the real messages being transmitted by telephone to Portsmouth. To satisfy interested observers, normal HQ traffic entered and left the phoney headquarters, including actor Clifton James, to whom was assigned the task of being Monty's double.

Field Marshal Gerd von Rundstedt, commander of the German Army in the west, was a staunch Calais believer. His subordinate, Field Marshal

Erwin Rommel, was just as firm an opponent of the theory. To von Rundstedt, there was no alternative which made military logic. The crossing fulfilled all the requirements for a seaborne invasion, but Rommel argued that this was probably the best reason for the Allies not choosing Dover/Calais for the crossing. The planners of *Fortitude* were delighted when word reached them that Rommel, opponent of the Calais theory, had mentioned in May that location of Montgomery's headquarters in Kent indicated the operational centre would be in south- eastern England. This was the first sign of a possible change in Rommel's opinion.

With an invasion imminent, radio traffic and other activity through the headquarters could be expected to increase, and the commanding General would be very much in evidence. So, with the approach of D-Day, the volume of activity gradually lessened. Towards the end of May, less than a fortnight before the planned date of landings, "Montgomery" alias Clifton James, well rehearsed for the part, resplendent in general's uniform, complete with shoe lifts as worn by Montgomery, left Britain for Gibraltar, where he was driven to Government House to meet the Governor who happened to be an old friend of the real Montgomery. In a Gibraltar alive with German agents, Montgomery-James spoke openly of *Plan 303*, an operation supposedly to take place near the south of France. Following his brief visit, James flew to Algiers, again openly and convincingly playing the part of the 21st Army Group Commander.

Montgomery's opposite, in almost every way, was George Patton. United States' General Patton, flamboyant, brash and incisive, an exponent of the fast advance, referred to by Hitler as the "cowboy general". Patton's troops had been the victors in Sicily, and Montgomery had defeated Rommel at El Alamein, so choice of Patton as Montgomery's co-invasion leader was, to the Germans, a logical action. Monitoring radio traffic through Montgomery's "headquarters" near Dover, they learned that Patton had been appointed to lead the US 3rd Army, so to them, with Patton's profile far ahead of the 1st Army's more retiring Lt Gen Omar

Bradley, Patton's 3rd Army had to be the invasion force. With formation of this unit known to be still in its infancy, obviously any invasion was not imminent.

Logic had to be admitted. If an invasion was to take place, surely the Commander's headquarters would be close to the point of departure. Montgomery's headquarters were near Dover, and this placed it, with other evidence, as the likely point of embarkation. If the invasion was to take place soon, it was hardly likely the commander would be away, soaking up the Gibraltar sun, hob-nobbing with his mates, then touring the Middle East. It was even more unlikely his equivalent Allied commander (Patton), would not have his troops trained and ready. No, the invasion was not going to occur for some time, and if it did, the odds were still well in favour of a landing at Calais, where fifteen German Divisions lay in wait.

Patton's role was to become evident later, in the Battle of Normandy, when, with a lightning thrust down the Atlantic Coast of West Contentin Peninsula, through Avranches, and with his 4th Armoured Division bursting out over the bridge at Pontaubault, Patton applied *Blitzkreig* to the inventors. Booming in two prongs towards Brest on the right, and Paris on the left, Patton's armoured and infantry divisions covered ground with a devastating speed which inspired other Allied armies.

The courageous Resistance

Meantime, the French Resistance continued to supply data from throughout France. Troop deployment, regimental identification, state of supplies, mined areas, unmined areas, details of fortifications, and other defence intelligence continued to flow in. Even the arcs of fire and ranges of the defences were monitored through the Norman fishing fleets. The Bay of the Seine provides the greater part of France's seafood, and at a time when food was in short supply, fishing became an important source. Practice shoots by the batteries without warning would have endangered the fishermen and their escorts, so before each battery was tested, fishing activities within range were suspended. From a study of the area cleared before a battery was tested, a reasonably accurate picture could be drawn of both range and arc of fire, through the simple expedient of noting which areas were cleared of fishing boats.

Transmission of information was particularly swift. On May 10th, after an air raid the previous evening, Rommel visited the Morsalines Battery with its open emplacements housing six 155 mm guns of French manufacture. As Merville commanded *Sword Beach* on the eastern flank, so Morsalines commanded *Utah* in the west. It was an old, isolated battery, constructed in 1941.

Through the passage of time, it had become as one with the countryside and so perfectly camouflaged that protection through construction of a new concrete roof would have destroyed its invisibility. Despite probing bombing attacks, so well was it hidden that minimal damage had been caused. Leaving Morsalines, Rommel was driven to St Pierre Eglise, a distance of 10.5 miles (17 km), and by the time he arrived, the BBC foreign service was carrying a message especially for him, to the effect that the battery had been bombed the evening before, but they were glad that "Herr Rommel had been able to find his camouflaged property that morning!" Thousands of similar pieces of information came flowing in, and at considerable risk, as the average life expectancy of an active Resistance operator was barely six months.

This information was frequently followed up from the air, by photographic reconnaissance. Some areas signposted as mined, were photographed with cows peacefully grazing on their pastures, and noted accordingly. Of concern, and supported by the air reconnaissance photographs, were triangles of steel girders about 5 feet (1.5 metres) high, which were sprouting from fields and on the beaches. These defences, christened *Rommel's Asparagus*, or *Czech Hedgehogs*, on the beaches, and armed with mines, were intended to prevent landing craft reaching shore, by either spearing or blowing them up, and in the fields their objective was to tear the bellies out of any aircraft attempting to land, and particularly targeteted gliders.

Manufactured from French railway lines, copies were made in England and methods of removal by tank and bulldozer tested. Then someone recalled that a few French railways had used lines imported from the United States, which were of a heavier gauge. When this material was used, the process of removal was an entirely different matter, and more sophisticated methods had to be devised.

Have harbour, will travel

Meanwhile, a convoy of 60 old vessels, ranging from the French warship *Courbet* to ancient tramps, code named *Goosberry*, was to sail for the beaches to fulfil their collective role as a breakwater protecting the *Mulberry* caissons after the landing. Nose to tail, in predetermined order and positions, with numbers painted on their sides, they were to be scuttled with explosives fitted by specialists from HMS *Vernon*, the Navy's explosives establishment.

They lay in the northern ports of Oban and Methil receiving attention for their last voyages. There were to be five *Goosberry* breakwaters, one each at Ouistreham (*Sword*), Courseulles (*Juno*), Arromanches (*Gold*), Colleville sur Mer (*Omaha*), and Vierville (*Utah*). Two of them would protect *Mulberry A*, Colleville sur Mer, (*Omaha*) and *Mulberry B* at Arromanches, (*Gold*).

Giant concrete structures, code named *Mulberries*, and originally inspired by Prime Minister Churchill, were to be towed across the Channel and positioned to fulfil the dual tasks of sheltering the beaches and forming wharves for the unloading of supplies to be transported ashore over the floating roadways connecting the *Mulberries* with the beach.

The Dieppe disaster had taught the Allies a valuable lesson. Capturing a port would be expensive, and probably unsuccessful. To land the volume of troops, equipment and supplies through one channel would result in bottlenecks and thus invited disaster. The vulnerability of a landing force to weather, combined with the necessity to unload supplies, required ports, and as Lord Louis Mountbatten had declared, "if a port cannot be captured, we must take one with us". So the *Mulberries* were conceived.

The original plan was for breakwaters to be sunk offshore in 30 feet of water, and connected with the beach by floating roadways named *Whales*. When it was realised that a harbour fixed to the sea bed would be rendered useless for much of each day by the rise and fall of the 20 foot tides, having to be 50 feet high to avoid being submerged, prototypes of massive floating caissons were developed from a previous design, the 200 x 12 foot (61 x 3.6 m) *Lilos*. From this experience, the *Mulberries* developed. The first were constructed in the Thames and towed to Newhaven, where, tested in a storm off Weymouth Bay, they proved a success, and production of 145 bombardons, each weighing between 2,000 and 6,000 tons was achieved by a work force of 15,000 over a period of eight months.

Feeding the monster

Maintenance of supply is fundamental for any force, whether defending or advancing, and through *Mulberry*, a facility for landing boxed supplies and mobile equipment had been established. But in fuelling the large army, at one time running at a vehicle to person ratio of 1:5, the Allies would have found their supplies choked through inability to deliver at the rate of consumption, if they employed conventional methods.

It was necessary to deliver direct, eliminate the delays of packaging, loading, unloading and delivering in drums to the consumers. PLUTO (Pipe Line Under The Ocean), was the ideal solution. First developed in early 1943, PLUTO consisted of a 3 inch flexible pipe wound around huge floating drums. The units, 70 miles in length, were towed across the Channel from the Isle of Wight, unwinding as they went, laying pipes through which fuel, water and oil would be pumped to Bort en Bessin, the initial point of distribution, and later to Cherbourg, with eventually more than 10 lines running from Dungeness to the Calais-Boulogne coast.

In Normandy, through the *Mulberries*, PLUTO, and the supply ships ready to ferry across the Channel, the Allies had their supply system arranged, and until May, so did the Germans, with a well planned rail and road network. In preference to the slow, grinding truck convoys, it was primarily the railways which fulfilled the requirement for fast, non stop movement of large quantities of goods and personnel, and it was upon the railways that the Allies turned their attention.

Destroying the German system

Still adhering to the two for one policy for Calais and Normandy, in late March the systematic elimination of railways in Northern France began. Destruction of rolling stock, marshalling yards, bridges and lines, began with a massive raid on Trappes, cutting the line between Paris and Chartres, with subsequent raids along the coast in which Amiens, Charleroi, Noisy and Bolougne received particular attention.

The raids were unrelenting, with fighter-bombers (Typhoons, Thunderbolts, Mustangs, Spitfires) augmenting the conventional bomber formations. In one day alone, more than 240 locomotives were claimed as destroyed or damaged by the 750 fighter-bombers which rampaged over the territory, firing with cannon and rocket, strafing and bombing anything that moved.

In the week from May 20th, 516 locomotives were claimed as damaged, and whilst some could be swiftly repaired and returned to operations, rail traffic in May was reduced to 55% of the January volume, and down to 30% at the beginning of June. Congestion and delays were the direct causes of many vital items not reaching their destinations by June the 6th. The mislaid or delayed armoured shields for the Crisbeq battery being one example, the ammunition and guns for Merville, another.

The material damage was, in many instances, secondary to the psychological. The Typhoon 1B, equipped with 8-60 lb rockets, bombs and 4 Hispano 20 mm cannon, was a particularly volatile anti tank weapon and an efficient eliminator of trains and road convoys. Night was the only time the enemy could take to the roads. By day it was suicide. Although trains were confined to their rails, tanks and road vehicles tried to hedge hop across fields but their tracks on the new ground were dead giveaways, and the fighter-bombers pounced.

On the roads, vehicles were sitting ducks, and smoking wreckage jammed the narrow carriageways, causing congestion and delays. Bridges, railway junctions, roads and repair facilities were ferociously attacked by these highly efficient weapon platforms, a payback in devastating terms for the activities of the once dreaded, but vulnerable, German JU87 (*Stuka*) dive bomber.

As an indication of the fighter-bomber's efficiency, the aircraft required less than one-quarter the weight of bombs to cause the same damage as a conventional high level bomber. A figure of approximately 650 tons from high level was considered necessary to destroy an average bridge, but a fighter-bomber required only 150 tons. The inefficiency of high level, so-called "carpet bombing", was demonstrated by the relative ease with which coastal targets were able to continue operation despite the most intensive bomber attack.

In the words of Air Marshal Arthur "Bomber" Harris, in describing heavy bomber involvement in the lead-up, and on D-Day itself . . ."In no circumstances could it be relied upon to destroy gun emplacements or cause noticeable casualties . . . nor is the heavy bomber force suitable for cutting railway communications at definite points . . . the only efficient support we (Bomber Command), can give to *Overlord* is the intensification of attacks on industrial centres in Germany".

However, Harris was not entirely correct. An anxious Prime Minister,

Winston Churchill, fearful of severe French civilian casualties in target areas should Harris' opinion concerning the lack of accuracy and precision of heavy area bombing prove valid, agreed in March to test the theory with a raid on five French towns, with the railway system at Vaires the principal target. It was completely successful, with the railway yards destroyed, and coincided with the arrival of a trainload of mines and a number of troop trains transporting Waffen SS troops of the Frundsberg division. The combination of high explosive, both aerial, and in their own mines, ripped through the trains, causing more than 3,000 casualties. Harris subsequently agreed to lend the facilities of Bomber Command to *Overlord*, and Lancasters particularly, played a significant role in pre-invasion softening up, D-Day itself, and the subsequent Battle of Normandy.

Allied aircraft ranged over northern and central France, wreaking damage on an enormous scale. As diversions, bridges over rivers totally unconnected with Allied plans were destroyed. Bridges along the Seine and radar emplacements were randomly attacked, and from mid-May, all airfields were thoroughly worked-over, causing the Luftwaffe to further diminish their effectiveness by removing already depleted forces further inland. In April and May, Bomber Command spent two-thirds of their time in the air over France, dropping 48,000 tons of bombs, increasing in June to 51,000 tons. General Doolittle's US 8th Air Force pounded the synthetic fuel plants at Bohlen, Chemnitz, Leuna, Zeitz, Zwickau, and later, the hydrogenation plant at Troglitz, reducing avgas output by 90% – a loss that was to rise to 98% by the end of July. Other fuels produced by the plants were similarly affected, severely restricting the movement of German transport and armoured units.

Between January and May, the Luftwaffe lost 30% of their fighter pilots each month. In this period, 2,262 fighters were lost from a total fighter pilot strength of 2,283, a rate of 99%. In May they suffered their most disastrous result, with 27% of twin engined, and 50.4% of single engined fighters being either lost or becoming unserviceable. Arising from the raids on fuel plants, pilot training schools, already harassed by sorties from long range allied fighters which shot down trainees before they even reached operational capability, were forced by fuel shortages to close, thus removing any possible replacement of pilots.

The raids had a secondary impact, that of compelling the fighter force to defend the installations, in the process suffering considerable losses to their already depleted numbers. The German war machine was in deep trouble. With production resources strangled, fuel for factories was short, and apart from the constant pounding from bombing raids on these factories, aircraft, truck, armament and all other production was winding down through lack of fuel.

But it was not all one sided. Between April and D-Day, the Allies lost slightly less than 2,000 aircraft and 12,000 men. In two days of the raids on the fuel production plants alone, the United States 8th lost 84 bombers, with the 8th and 15th Air Forces losing 409 aircraft in April – more aircraft and crews than it had ever lost, or would in the future.

Buildup

The departure timetable for *Overlord* would begin with the sailing of the *Gooseberrys* from their northern ports, then despatch of Forces U and O, followed by the remainder of the fleet for assembly at *Piccadilly Circus*, coded *Area Z*.

In sequence, the Air Forces were to saturate allocated defence emplacements with bombs, parachute and glider borne troops were to land shortly after midnight, destroy selected defence positions, complete the capture of key bridges and towns, holding them until relieved.

In the early hours of D-Day, a naval bombardment of defensive positions was to be conducted by more than 28 vessels, the register of which read as a Who's Who of warships. Battleships USS *Arkansas, Nevada, Texas*, HMS

Ramillies and *Warspite*, cruisers HMS *Ajax*[1] and HMS *Belfast*[2], HMS *Arethusa, Argonaut, Danae, Diadem, Emerald, Frobisher, Glasgow, Hawkins, Orion*, the French cruisers *Montcalm* and *Georges Leygues*, USS cruisers *Tuscaloosa* and *Quincy*, the Polish cruiser *Dragon*, the Dutch sloops *Flores* and *Soemba*, supported by destroyers HMS *Black Prince, Hawkins* and *Enterprise*, and the monitors HMS *Erebus* and USS *Roberts*.

These were the vessels with assigned targets, apart from those with specific escort and support bombardment roles. The United States was fighting two wars simultaneously, and the massive resources of that country were divided between Europe, and the Pacific conflict, whilst Britain's naval strength was principally concentrated upon the war in Europe, and so British vessels predominated.

Each unit of the naval forces was assigned specific targets, a time to open fire and a time to cease fire. The ceasefire time was co-ordinated so the barrage would lift as the landing craft approached the beaches, the objective being to provide a window between the barrage lifting too late and so endangering the Allies' own troops, but not too soon so the defenders were provided with recovery time and the opportunity to re-man their weapons. Each of the first wave assault units was to land at precise times to fill the window between the barrage ceasing and the defenders' recovery.

Over the period of nine months, aerial reconnaissance had built up a complete photographic record of the corridors inland to Paris, Berlin and

---

1 Battle of the River Plate, in which the comparatively lightly armed cruisers, *Ajax, Achilles* and *Exeter* severely damaged the German pocket battleship *Admiral Graf Spee* forcing her captain (Captain Hans Langsdorff) to scuttle the vessel. Langsdorff subsequently committed suicide in preference to the Court Martial which awaited him in Germany. *Ajax's* guns were knocked out in the battle and Commodore Harwood ordered her withdrawal.

2 *Belfast* is anchored in the Thames, and open for public inspection throughout the week.

points in between, identifying features of the paths from each landing point, but as the designated day approached, the pace quickened. Intelligence operations responded to demands from commanders for up to date information, and in the two weeks before D-Day, one single photo processing unit produced more than 100,000 prints for the Army.

Across the entire span of the northern French coast, air reconnaissance increased in intensity, with aircraft crossing and re-crossing the coast, photographing from every angle, including an infantryman's eye view – a series of photographs taken from wavetop height approaching the beaches – and rising to 200, then 1,000 feet, photographing the land behind.

Each commander knew what was in front, near, and behind their assigned landing point, the defences, bridges, the terrain – rivers, hills, villages, narrow roads – and the hazards. From the maps and other intelligence smuggled by the Resistance from France to Britain, Allied knowledge of the enemy and their strength was generally more complete than the Germans' own.

Weapon strength and the placement of each gun, the beach defences, the range and arc of fire of the batteries, troop numbers, and even their unit identification, deployment, morale, quantity of supplies, ammunition, food reserves, even the composition and load bearing capacity of the sand on every beach, were known intimately.

The Plan was complete.

CHAPTER THREE

ASSEMBLY
AND DESPATCH

"Tense as a coiled spring" was the description given to the atmosphere in England where the entire southern area, from the east to the west coasts had been sealed off. Travel between Britain and Eire was banned. In more than 1,100 camps, in ports throughout the island nation, on the many airfields which, with the camps, seemed to occupy the British Isles, in villages and towns, in the cities and at sea, men and women waited for the signal.

The weather could hardly have been worse, with wind and rain lashing England and northern France, casting considerable doubt at Supreme Headquarters (SHAEF), as to whether the scheduled June 5th landing could go ahead as planned.

Operation Neptune, the naval phase of *Overlord*, involved 6,840 ships segmented into 47 convoys. Poised, ready to go were 160,000 troops and their equipment, 15,000 aircraft, the special assignment paratroopers and commandos, and to lead *Neptune* were 6 battleships, followed by 23 cruisers, 122 destroyers, 450 escorts, including mine-sweepers, and thousands of torpedo boats, cargo vessels and landing craft.

The wait

Gathered in Britain's north-western ports were the *Gooseberrys*, the fleet of old ships, lead by the liner *Durban*, intended to form breakwaters for five landing sites at Ouistreham, Courseulles, Arromanches, St Laurent and Varreville sur Mer. For six months, the vessels had been in the process of preparation for their last voyages, and now fitted with their demolition charges, they waited in Oban and Methil for the order to sail.

Waiting also were the *Mulberries*, giant hollow concrete caissons or bombardons, the size of small skyscrapers, to be towed across the Channel and form artificial floating harbours, *Mulberry A* off Colleville sur Mer, and *Mulberry B* at Arromanches.

The midget submarines, *X20*, (Lt Ken Hudspeth RANVR) and *X23*, (Lt George Honour RNVR), were ready to begin their task of marking the perimeters of the British-Canadian sector. Based at Fort Blockhouse at Gosport, from which they were used to survey the French beaches and obtain soil samples, the small submarines were no strangers to that coastline. Their function was to arrive the day before D-Day, submerge off their allotted beaches and wait, *X20* in the shallows off the small town of Courseulles, and *X23*, 20 miles away, similarly positioned off Ouistreham at the mouth of the Orne.

On the signal that the invasion was to begin, their task was to activate sonar apparatus which broadcast a homing signal to guide the fleet shorewards. As an addition, each mounted a light directed out to sea, and visible only to incoming craft. As protection, the small craft were to fly large yellow flags, just like the buoys at Cowes week, except they also made easily identifiable targets for enemy artillery.

On the airfields, troops, pilots, equipment and their transport, rows of Hamilcar, Waco and Horsa gliders and their C47 tugs (also known as Dakotas, or Douglas DC3s), lined up in rows. Other airfields were occupied by fighter escorts, bombers, and the Lancasters which were to distribute "chaff" (or "window"); strips of foil which, fluttering down, were intended to confuse the remaining enemy radar.

All D-Day aircraft, including gliders, were soon to receive a last minute treatment of three broad bands of white striping to wings and fuselages. Planned well beforehand, the paint was applied within the last 10 hours to minimise the opportunity for German reconnaissance to detect the new markings and either duplicate to confuse, or realise that a new development was about to occur.

The timetable was to begin with despatch of the *Gooseberry* fleet, departure of shipping for the Channel assembly and despatch point (*Piccadilly Circus*, or *Area Z*), an increase in bomber activity directed towards strategic targets, followed by the pathfinders parachuting in to Normandy to mark target and drop zones for glider and paratroop landings at Benouville and on the Contentin Peninsula. The beach assaults were to begin with sea bombardment of land targets, the troop landings, establishment of beachheads, then the artificial ports, followed up by landings of reinforcements and supplies, and the laying of the PLUTO pipelines.

The beginning

And still the weather remained foul, with winds causing 6 foot (2 m) waves in the Channel, but plans had to proceed on the assumption that *Overlord* would begin on schedule. There was now no room for last minute decisions or improvisation. The machine was winding up, and the first move began with the June 2nd departure for Normandy of the two X-Craft, behind their towing submarine, HMS *Sapper*. In the evening twilight, quietly moving from their Portsmouth moorings under their own power, the two ghosted away to rendezvous with their tug and escort of two armed trawlers at sea off the port, beginning *Operation Gambit*. After initial difficulties in linking up, the little fleet moved off towards France, moving with difficulty in the boisterous conditions, until the tows were slipped shortly before dawn.

From here, they were without support, but for *X20's* Ken Hudspeth, isolation, and the resourcefulness this demanded, was not new. As commander of *X10* in September 1943, he spent eight days navigating his

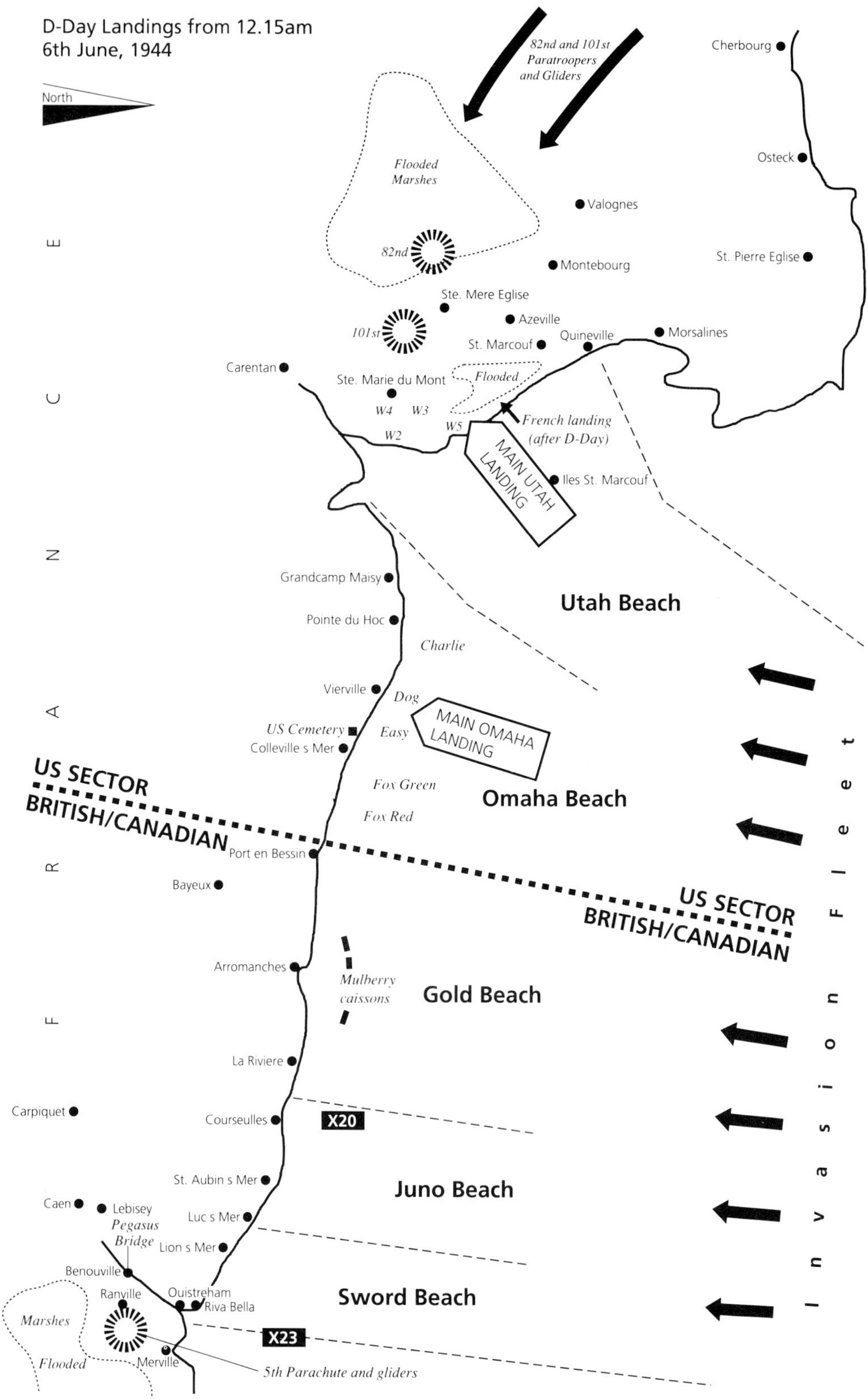
D-Day Landings from 12.15am
6th June, 1944
North
F R A N C E
82nd and 101st
Paratroopers
and Gliders
Cherbourg
Osteck
Flooded
Marshes
Valognes
82nd
Montebourg
St. Pierre Eglise
Ste. Mere Eglise
Azeville
101st
St. Marcouf
Quineville
Morsalines
Carentan
Flooded
Ste. Marie du Mont
W4
W3
W2
W5
French landing
(after D-Day)
MAIN UTAH
LANDING
Iles St. Marcouf
Grandcamp Maisy
Utah Beach
Pointe du Hoc
Charlie
Vierville
Dog
MAIN OMAHA
LANDING
US Cemetery
Easy
Colleville s Mer
Fox Green
Omaha Beach
Fox Red
US SECTOR
BRITISH/CANADIAN
Port en Bessin
Bayeux
US SECTOR
BRITISH/CANADIAN
I n v a s i o n F l e e t
Arromanches
Mulberry
caissons
Gold Beach
La Riviere
Carpiquet
Courseulles
X20
St. Aubin s Mer
Juno Beach
Caen
Lebisey
Pegasus
Bridge
Luc s Mer
Lion s Mer
Benouville
Ranville
Ouistreham
Riva Bella
Sword Beach
Marshes
X23
Flooded
Merville
5th Parachute and gliders

partially crippled craft through Norwegian fjords during the midget submarine attacks against *Scharnhorst* and *Tirpitz* in Altenfjord and Kaafjord, finally meeting the tow submarine, HMS *Stubborn* at a last resort rendezvous, with half an hour to spare.

Now, both submerged, and travelling towards the French coast, they remained that way until evening, when surfaced, and with batteries charging, the submarines continued until the early hours of Sunday morning, by which time with the coast visible, each submerged opposite the position they judged to be their respective parking areas.

The French resistance in Normandy was to be alerted with the first line of the French Poet, Paul Verlaine's poem *Chanson d'Automne (Song of Autumn). Les sanglots longs des violins de l'automne (the long sobs of the violins of autumn)* was transmitted on the 1st of June, intercepted and recorded by the Germans, many of whom were still were sceptical. The second part, to notify the invasion would take place within 24 hours, *Blessent mon couer d'une langueur monotone (wound my heart with a monotonous langour)*, followed at 9.15 pm, 10.20 and 10.15 pm on the evening of the 5th and was also intercepted. Still the significance of the messages was not taken seriously, and the log at von Runstedt's HQ was noted "of course nothing will happen".

Another blunder

In England, an Associated Press teletype operator, practising with hypothetical news releases, types out: *Urgent: Associated Press NYK Flash – Eisenhower HQ announced Allied landings in France.* The tape is not erased, and goes out with the Russian bulletins. Even swift corrective action is too late, and the release is picked up and broadcast by Radio Berlin and Radio Moscow. At Lieutenant Colonel Helmuth Meyer's 15th Army intelligence HQ at Pas-de-Calais, the *Flash* is recorded, but causes little concern. There had been too many false alarms, and there was no activity on the coast.

At this time, the second line of *Chanson d'Automne* had not been broadcast, but even if the most senior commanders were cynical of the Verlaine connection, German Intelligence was not. It was a message well known throughout the Resistance, and consequently through Abwehr (German Intelligence) contacts within the French underground. Admiral Canaris, head of the Abwehr, had singled this out as being the most reliable indication of an imminent invasion. No second line had been transmitted. The *Flash* was discarded.

Foul weather continues

General Eisenhower had ordered the despatch of Forces U and O, his thought being that if there was a chance the gale would drop, the fleet would be running to schedule for a 5th of June landing. By dawn of the 4th, it was obvious the weather was not moderating. The passage across would be miserable, with troops cold, seasick, and in no condition to assault the heavily defended beaches, that is, if they were able to reach them through the surf. Equipment would be lost, and the entire operation placed in peril. The weather was just too bad, and the risk to men and equipment, and success of the whole operation too great.

Recall signals went out to Force U which was at sea, and part of Force O, although Force 2A did not receive the order, and ploughed on towards the rendezvous point. Destroyers and aircraft were despatched to head it off and return the convoy to port. Tomorrow the weather may moderate, but tomorrow and the following day were the last possible times when moon and tides were right for another month. The decision had been made that the crossing should be by moonlight and the landing in daylight, but tides were another vital consideration, and tides were only suitable on six days in June. Of these, only three coincided with moonlight.

All day Sunday, and in the evening, with the weather worsening, the

X-Craft and their crews lay on the sea bed, until at 1am, Monday June 5th they surfaced, tuned their radios to 1850 kc and awaited the signal. It came – *Padfoot*, *Padfoot*, *Padfoot*, and the crews knew the landing was not to be the 5th. Postponed 24 hours, and another day of waiting lay ahead.

The absent Generals

In France, German commanders received their weather forecasts, looked at the blowing trees, the rain and surf, concluding there would be no invasion tonight. Troops were stood down and senior officers went their separate ways, Rommel had already left on the 4th[1] and was in Germany with his wife for her birthday, taking with him a pair of hand made shoes as a present.

Various Normandy commanders, Lt Gen Heinz Hellmich, commander of the division which occupied one part of the Cherbourg Peninsula, Maj Gen Wilhelm Falley, Col Wilhelm Meyer-Detring, Lt Gen Karl von Schlieben and others were to take part in a mapping and war games conference at Rennes on the 6th, so early departures for the city were planned. One by one they arrived, placing them 95 road miles (150 km) from the Normandy drop zones. The theme of the exercise was a theoretical and very speculative *Kriegspiel* based on a mythical sea and airborne landing.

The theoretical location, Normandy.

In addition, other key officers who were not to participate in the conference were absent from their commands, and at midnight of the 5th, 15 minutes before the first pathfinders parachuted in, Major Gen Erich Marcks, commander of the German 84th Corps at St Lô, cut the birthday cake his staff had arranged. The message issued by the 7th Army's chief of staff, warning them not to leave their commands before dawn, arrived too late.

1 *Army Group B War Diary*

That evening, lawyer Michel Hardelay was probably wondering whether his villa, on the seafront of what was soon to become *Omaha Beach*, would be there tomorrow evening. As the Germans tunnelled into the hillsides and constructed their fortifications, building materials were required, and the closest materials were in the structures of the colourful little seaside villas which lined the shore. Once, there had been ninety of them, now only seven remained, and Hardelay's was to be demolished tomorrow, the 6th of June.

Agonising

In England, the day before, General Eisenhower had agonised over a decision he had to make within half an hour, a decision which was being forced upon him by a combination of weather, obligations to others – the Resistance being one, where thousands of people had received their alerts, and were waiting – and the momentum of an expectation which spread throughout the waiting invasion force, an expectation which could not be sustained much longer without seriously impacting morale.

Cooped up in camps, in ships, sitting in their tanks, lorries or jeeps, the men waited. Some had been travelling since May 26th and on their landing craft from Wednesday, the 31st. With an Admiralty gale warning issued on Sunday morning, conditions for the men were barely tolerable. Some, already seasick, ate seasickness pills and vomited into their helmets. Toilet systems were overflowing, and everyone was wet, miserable and fed up. Morale was at rock bottom, men of the US 1st Army were making noises about wanting to go home, and any further delay would have been catastrophic.

Twenty thousand vehicles, more than 157,000[2] troops, harbours and bays crammed with ships, some at wharves five and six abreast, trains loaded with

2 Eventually to total 2 million landed through Normandy.

troops and supplies, and still more coming into the area, all waiting. Queues of transport, armaments, supplies and materials backed up on roads and railway lines, troops suffering from the weather, cramped conditions, a mixture of congestion, boredom, anxiety and apprehension.

Decision

At 9.30 am on that grey Sunday, with rain lashing the windows of the library of Southwick House, and cloud scudding overhead, General Eisenhower called a meeting of senior staff. Air Chief Marshals Tedder and Leigh-Mallory, General Montgomery, Major-General Walter Bedell-Smith, Admiral Ramsay, gathered the hear the latest forecast from a concerned RAF meteorologist, Group Captain Stagg. The minimum conditions required; calm, with a cloud base above 3,000 feet, and at least 3 miles visibility, did not exist, and all looked to Stagg for some hope.

There was a possibility of a short window of relative calm, he said, with a clearing pattern moving in from the Atlantic, along the Channel, rain ceasing, cloud clearing sufficiently for bombing operations to be effective, and winds lessening. This break would probably last throughout the 5th, and on the morning of the 6th, but from then on, the picture was not promising, with the likely renewal of gusty, rainy conditions.

With fuel problems for the Navy if a delay occurred, landing on the 7th was no longer an option. A period of debate followed, with some in favour of postponement, others advocating a landing on the 6th – particularly Sir Bernard Montgomery, with the forceful response, "I say go . . . go!"

For a number of minutes, Eisenhower, head bowed, thought. For now the decision, one which would affect the futures of millions, lay with him. The group waited. Eventually, he looked up, still worried, and said "I don't like it, but there it is. I don't see how we can possibly do anything else, I'm positive we must give the order". Tuesday was to be D-Day.

The meeting had occupied a shade over 15 minutes.

The spring unwinds

On May 30th, the aged ships which formed the *Gooseberry* blockship fleet, had put to sea from their northern ports. With the naval officer commanding, in *Sumatra*, carrying separate orders for the alternative dates of 5th or 6th of June, *Sumatra*, and the other fifty-nine vessels, the *Gooseberrys*, headed for the Bristol Channel.

Monday morning, and Forces J (*Juno*), G (*Gold*), had sailed, whilst Forces U and O (*Utah* and *Omaha*) were back at sea again. In poor weather conditions, with winds gusting to more than 20 knots generating waves of 6 feet (2 m) and more, the invasion fleet sailed for the rendezvous point, *Area Z*, or *Piccadilly Circus*. From this circle in the ocean, 25 miles (40 km) off the coast of Portsmouth, the Forces, with the exception of U, which short-cut in from the West, would peel off to follow the five channels which widened out to ten buoy marked lanes, one for slow traffic, one for fast, leading them to their allocated landing beaches.

In the largest precision minesweeping exercise of the war, a fleet of 300 minesweepers moved ahead, clearing a 15 mile (24 km) channel at the start, which doubled in width at its end. Proceeding in ranks essential for effective sweeping, the vessels moved without air cover and, being locked in to a particular formation and course, hampered by their sweeps, would have been unable to take evasive action in the event of attack. In the broad daylight of June 5th, they drew closer to a hostile coast, a coast still very much alive and deadly, as the planned softening up operations were not to fully come into operation for a further twelve hours.

However, nothing occurred. No enemy reconnaissance aircraft, no E or S Boats out of Cherbourg or Le Havre disturbed their work, and by 9 pm that evening, with some of the small vessels in sight of Normandy, their work was complete. Still not an aircraft, ship or shore battery indicated they had been spotted.

That afternoon, 126 aircraft of the German 26th Wing departed Normandy for airfields further east, leaving only two of their number behind. Only 35 fighters now remain within striking distance of the invasion area, and three-quarters are reported to be unserviceable.

Mid Channel, the vast armada which was to end the German occupation of France, bore down on the coast. Warships of every size and description, from battleships to MTBs; their task to fulfil bombardment or escort duties. Landing craft, plodding tramps, hospital and supply vessels, all heading towards their assigned positions, adhering to a precise timetable, requiring a navigational accuracy which permitted no error.

The final BBC French service messages for the Resistance were being transmitted. *It is hot in Suez; The tomatoes should be picked; The dice are on the table; Soothe my heart with a monotonous langour* . . . Some genuine, others included to confuse, but the genuine messages meant something to different Resistance units. Meyer immediately contacted von Runstedt, his staff dismissing the matter as a false alarm, as it was considered unlikely that Eisenhower would announce his impending arrival by radio. Thus, when it counted, the Verlaine message was disregarded.

Contrary to an understanding with the Free French in Britain, who wished only those members of the Resistance near the point of entry to be activated, (but not a good idea, as it would give away the location), all messages were transmitted.

Across France, members of the Maquis will begin their tasks of sabotage, and the enemy will still not know where the landing is to be. Again, some lives are being sacrificed to save others.

To mask the activity now occurring, a diversion planned a month ago, swung into action. Involving a small group of Lancasters from 617 Squadron[3], commanded by Col Leonard Cheshire, and augmented with

3   The famous "Dam Buster" squadron, which in May 1943, in a low level operation which required the aircraft to be maintained at a height of 60 feet and constant speed and direction, bombed the Ruhr dams using the unique Barnes Wallis "Bouncing bombs".

Stirling bombers of 218 Squadron, the task of the aircraft was to slowly fly back and forth, releasing a steady stream of foil strips, which slowly fluttered down, providing a wall of confusion for enemy radar. Gradually proceeding along the Channel in the general direction of Calais, the aircraft continued to dispense their "chaff" whilst below, a flotilla of small vessels towing barrage balloons, provided simulation for radar of a fleet of large warships.

Cheshire's pilots were masters of precision. It was 617 which used Lancasters as dive-bombers to accurately mark targets with incendiaries, and it was 617 which was accorded one of the precision jobs of the invasion, that of moving a phantom fleet at the pace of ships, up the Channel from aircraft moving at ten times that speed.

Now, from Newbury airfield, C47 Dakotas, and from Harwell, RAF Albermarle aircraft take off with their cargoes of pathfinders to be dropped over the paratroop and glider landing zones of Ranville and near Ste Mere Eglise.

Along the coast, from Calais to Cherbourg, heavy bombers were pounding defences, still following the two-for-one ratio of two bombs for Calais to every one for Normandy. At 11.30 pm, the 1,000 Bomber command aircraft began their assault, dropping 5,800 bombs on defence positions from La Pernelle in the West to Houlgate in the east. Midnight was approaching, and tomorrow would be part of history.

On the evening of May 31st, ten sonic lane marking buoys were positioned to mark the run-in entrances to the five beaches. With signals timed to activate on June the 4th, and operate within an eight hour span on each day until the 10th of June, they transmitted on navigational frequencies. From the 5th of June, they were backed up by ten HDMLs of the 149th HDML Flotilla, commanded by Lt Lloyd Hargraves RANVR, which attached themselves to each buoy. The small launches left Devonport on the 4th in atrocious weather conditions, and with the postponement, were recalled, slogging their way back home. Next morning, they headed to sea again, mooring to their respective buoys at midnight, each directing an infra red light seawards. In 15 minutes, the first paratroops would land in Normandy.

D-Day had arrived.

Omaha Beach June 1944

This scene was almost constant all the way along the coast, with people and supplies streaming ashore at the secured beach heads.

The photograph on page 54 is the reverse of this, looking uphill, and was taken from an approximate position to the left of the photo on the cross track. This is now the seafront roadway with a low wall separating it from the sand, at about the level of the closest beached vessel. Barrage balloons, intended to deter an almost non-existent Luftwaffe, acted as effective markers for German artillery, and thus were frequently cut adrift. (USNA 192599)

Pegasus Bridge, 6th June 1944. Major Howard's gliders

Cairns mark the approximate landing areas, Benouville, 6th June 1993

War and peace. A Bren carrier crossing Pegasus Bridge, June 1944

After the memorial service, 11 am, 6th June 1993

Utah Beach landings, 1944, 1 km west of *Strongpoint W5* 53

Utah Beach, June 1993. Nothing changes

54 — *Omaha Beach* breakout, June 1944

Omaha breakout, June 1993

The Hardelay villa, 6th June 1993

Section of *Utah Beach*. This distance had to be covered under fire during landings at low tide

56 Pointe du Hoc. Cliffs scaled by the US 2nd Ranger Battalion

Grassed and tended, but the craters remain 50 years afterwards

Going home. Mme Audiee Digeon after her release from German detention, 6th June 1944   57

The same location, N14 flyover, Ste Mere Eglise, June 1993

Crisbeq, in US hands, 11th June 1944

Damage was caused after capture. Photo, June 1992

Crisbeq rubble, hamlet and the coast June 1944

June 1993

60 Ste Mere Eglise, intersection of the N13 highway (across the photograph), June 1944

Ste Mere Eglise, road to the sea, 1993

Ste Mere Eglise, 1992. Effigy of the paratrooper Pte John Steele 61

Many coastal roads in Normandy bear the names of servicemen who paid the supreme sacrifice

62   A sunken D-Day breakwater backgrounds today's Norman mussel farmers, June 1993

Terrain which caused so many problems between June and August 1944

CHAPTER FOUR

LANDINGS
DIVISION OF TERRITORY

Through the ages, the course of battles, however well planned, have frequently failed to turn out the way their planners intended, and many a general or admiral has stood helpless as rain has bogged an army, snow has frozen his troops, waves, tide, or a change of wind has altered the course of a conflict on the sea.

In 1944, it was no different, as wind, waves, cloud, tide and flood worked to defeat the invading allies, as tanks designed to swim were swamped, carrying their crews to the bottom. Landing craft broached in the surf, striking the mines their commanders sought so desperately to avoid, and the beaches, long and flat at low tide, were hailed with bullets and shrapnel through which the incoming troops had to run.

Cloud and wind, combined with enemy flak, disoriented the pilots of aircraft towing gliders or transporting parachutists, so the gliders cast off in the wrong area, or the pilots of the transport aircraft discharged their cargoes inaccurately, and parachutists came down miles from their intended targets, many drowning with their heavy equipment in the flooded marshes and rivers.

Tide, wind and waves carried landing craft away from their planned targets, in some instances luckily, in others, with disastrous results. Vital supplies landed far away, and were lost. Some fell into enemy hands, and apart from military equipment, German troops enjoyed an unexpected feast of coffee, condensed milk, biscuits, tinned pineapple and other delicacies they had not seen for years.

The minutely planned softening up process by naval bombardment, was in most instances extremely accurate, and the follow up support where destroyers swept in close to land and picked off pockets of resistance which were causing inconvenience, assisted the land forces enormously. Each of the vessels had an allocated target, and knew just about all there was to know about it – strength, types of guns, construction, field of fire, range of the guns, and in many instances, even the morale of men was known from the intelligence which had built up, including information as recent as photographs taken only a few days beforehand.

Aerial bombing, intended to pulverise defences, often missed the target by a large margin, supporting Air Chief Marshal Harris' original opinion. The ability of defenders to weather an onslaught and re-emerge amongst churned up earth and wreckage to carry on the fight was astounding.

Guns which the allies expected to be installed in the German batteries were, in some instances, not fitted, senior German officers were absent from their commands, and the weather was terrible. Overriding all, the German High Command refused to believe the invasion was actually taking place. So effective had been *Fortitude*, that nothing could shake their belief in Pas-de-Calais. Consolidating this belief was the volume of bombing which had been sustained over the previous week and the two for one policy which was still followed faithfully.

The Lancasters and Stirlings with the little fleet vessels towing barrage balloons, and other diversionary tactics such as *Rupert*, the parachutist dummy which exploded with firecracker noise on contact with the ground, inclined them to consider any activity, unless Calais – related, to be a diversion. *Rupert*, even when discovered, puzzled the finders, causing confusion and delay, further complicating the picture.

He was a little fellow, two to three feet (62-93cm) in height and dressed to resemble a paratrooper. On contact with the ground, he set off a series of rapid explosions, which approximated the sound of gunfire sufficiently to cause considerable alarm in German headquarters. For some hours, the thought was that paratroopers had landed at Lessay, 19 miles (30 km) from the actual drop zones.

Weeks of bombing had all but pulverised the railway system, and the Resistance was now hard at work completing the job. Ammunition and building materials for the batteries, the guns themselves, steel acoustic mines for harbours, food and other supplies were either in wrecked trains standing in sidings waiting for track repairs or a spare engine, or had not even left the factory. The only alternative was road transport, but this was slow and inefficient. Convoys were prime targets for the fighter-bombers, and convoy debris littered the roads, further choking the transport system. If trucks attempted to go across country, they were caught in the open and just as effectively destroyed.

Allied as the forces may have been, there still existed obvious divisions between the two principal nations, the United States and Great Britain. The geographical assignment of the landing beaches, with the two United States main beaches, *Utah* and *Omaha* to the west, and their secondary landing, Pointe du Hoc sandwiched between, next the British beaches of *Gold* as their western flank, and *Sword* to the east, with the Canadian beach, *Juno* in the middle, illustrated the specific demarcation of the invasion territory. America was to the west, Britain and Canada to the east.

Then add in the support operation, with American paratroopers and glider borne troops landing behind *Utah*, the US Air Force conducting the bombing assault along the *Utah-Omaha* stretch, and all available US naval forces, supported by British, French and Dutch warships bombarding the same beaches. In the British-Canadian sector, Royal Air Force aircraft bombed the *Gold-Juno-Sword* sector, the Royal Navy with one Polish, and one Dutch warship shelled the same area. Units of the

RN and RAF also provided services for the joint operation, where the 149th HDML flotilla marked the sonar buoys, and the Lancaster-Stirling combination with the small launches and their barrage balloons, created a phantom fleet diversion for the benefit of German radar.

The weather continued to be poor, with wind and a channel chop. On land, unpredictable gusts were to have a disastrous effect upon aircraft, gliders and paratroop landings, placing a number of well planned operations in peril.

First action

In mid channel, the diversionary operation involving the tinsel "chaff" (or "window") methodically sprinkled by the Lancasters of 617 Squadron and Stirlings of 218, was in full swing. With the small fleet towing barrage balloons to simulate large ships plodding towards Cap d'Antifer, the aircraft ran 35 seconds forward, retracing their course for 32 seconds, then back again for 35 seconds over a two hour shift, changing with the relief aircraft which had 3 seconds to slip into position. There were four of these two hour shifts. The radar stations still operating, reported activity in the Channel, and confusion on their screens, but no hint of the fleet moving towards Normandy.

The Albermarles and C47s droned on, heading for their pathfinder drop zones, and close behind were the gliders and tugs transporting Major John Howard's Benouville assault team from the Oxford and Buckinghamshire Light Infantry, and the US 101st and 82nd Airborne Divisions which were to land near Sainte Mere Eglise.

In the three gliders, Howard's men waited for cast-off, when their craft would begin the slow spiral down to the grassy flats beside the canal, while the bomber tugs continued on for a short distance to bomb Caen as a value added, and further diversionary gesture. The gliders whispered towards the ground, seeming to increase in speed as the land approached, until at last came the bump and rumble as each careered across the grass, losing speed, until eventually spinning to a stop, they disgorged their contents, some troops exiting through fractures or through the nose, running towards their objective, on time, fifteen minutes past midnight.

The rumpus which the Albermarles were creating over Caen masked the noise of the gliders' landing, although on the bridge, a sentry thought he heard a sound, but assumed it may have been a crashing bomber. By the time the actual situation had been realised, Major Howard's men had overrun the perimeter defences, swarmed on to the bridge, and immediately checked it for demolition charges. So swift and unexpected had been their assault, that the bridge's explosive charges had not been wired, and it was retained intact. Only fifteen minutes had elapsed.

"Ham and Jam", code for capture of the bridge, was transmitted, and now it was a matter of Howard and his 150 men following the order to hold until relieved, and waiting until Brigadier Lord Lovat's 1st Special Service Brigade, landing at Ouistreham in the first wave on *Sword Beach*, reached the defenders, which they did, marching in to the tune of "Blue Bonnets". Benouville, the town across the bridge, was captured by Major General Richard Gale's 5th Parachute Brigade at 2 am, and the nearest building now claims to be the first house in France to be liberated .

Confusion

Accurate as Howard's gliders had been, the British pathfinders were not so fortunate. Through a combination of high winds, poor visibility, and evasive action by the pilots of their transports, they scattered. The blind drop into unfamiliar territory had been traumatic enough, but finding themselves on foreign ground and unable to orientate or recognise the terrain, caused chaos.

Parachutes supporting vital equipment blew away, teams of path-finders, dropped together, were caught by winds and separated. One team of ten lost six of their number as they were carried towards the flooded Dives and drowned. Other teams fell into their wrong areas and set up their code flashing systems where they landed, which of course transmitted a code which did not apply to that sector, or were forced to set up what directional equipment remained, away from their true targets. Some even dropped in to farmyards or the front gardens of buildings used as enemy command posts. Despite the difficulties, more than 60 pathfinders began their task of marking targets for the paratroopers who were to follow shortly after 1 am.

Merville

Now, it was Merville's turn. The battery which threatened beaches from Ouistreham to St Aubin sur Mer, had to be neutralised, and it was to Lt Col Terence Otway of the Royal Ulster Rifles and the 9th Battalion, 3rd Parachute Brigade that this responsibility had been allotted. The emplacement, with its 4-150 mm guns, was a key target, and had to be captured by 30 minutes before dawn.

At 12.30, 109 Lancaster bombers attacked the battery, conducting what was intended to be a saturation raid, using "blockbuster" bombs of up to two tons each. But the weather turned against them, and bombing through a low overcast, they missed the target by up to a mile, and in the process almost eliminated the advance ground party, an unplanned hazard which caused considerable consternation. In total, more than 380 tons of explosive rained down on the innocent village of Gonneville without a hit being recorded on the target.

Paratroopers who were to prepare the ground for the glider borne assault teams, arrived over their drop zones with little to indicate their accuracy, and forced by searchlights and heavy flak, to jink and swerve, pilots of the C47 aircraft became disoriented, discharging their cargo over a spread of more than 40 miles. The burning town was mistaken for the battery, and paratroopers were unloaded some distance from the correct objective. Worse, the gliders carrying heavy weapons, ammunition, and other equipment, including the explosives necessary to destroy Merville, were missing.

Of the original 700 men, a bare 150 remained, most of the others having been carried far inland over the flooded Dives Valley with its marshes and deep water filled ditches, where a man falling in, laden with a heavy pack, had little chance of survival. And of their equipment, there were no heavy guns, no mortars, no assault vehicles, nor were there mine detectors, or the sapper specialists to wire the explosives – but the explosives were missing anyway. Apart from one Vickers machine gun, and some lengths of Bangalore torpedo, the small party had only the equipment they carried in with them. So much for careful planning and rehearsals.

Although there was a backup plan, whereby HMS *Arethusa's* 6 inch guns would shell the area if a "captured" signal had not been received, the signalling equipment had also been lost, so it was decided that an attempt should be made despite the difficulties. Reaching their objective, the party crept inside the perimeter fence, attempting to locate each defensive position, moving to the inner wire.

Part of the plan was the arrival of three gliders, carrying assault teams and additional equipment, which were to crash land inside the perimeter after the main party had secured an area. Exactly on schedule, two arrived overhead at 4.25 am, the other having been forced to return to England. Now, seeking a ground signal, the pair circled, attempting to identify the landing area.

It was a signal the frustrated Otway could not give, for the equipment was amongst that lost earlier, and he watched helplessly as the aircraft circled, exposing themselves to the streams of fire that poured up from the emplacements. Turning away, one glider, perhaps mistaking the still burning Gonneville as the target, landed 3 miles distant, and the other came down in a field near the battery, where it was immediately engaged by German defences.

The decision was made to continue the assault, without the flamethrowers, scaling ladders, anti tank weapons, demolition charges, amplification, radio and signalling equipment, mortars and machine guns. And without even the specialist teams which should have arrived in the two gliders, but now had their own wars to fight, and of course without the 600 men who had scattered over an area of more than 50 square miles (130 sq km).

Bangalores blew the wire apart, Otway's men streamed through in what was thought to be a suicidal operation, but so intense and persistent was their fire, and desperate their action that within 30 minutes German gunners surrendered. It was 4.50 am[1] and the operation had been successful, but not without cost. Of the original 150 men, 70 were killed or wounded.

Then came the realisation that the guns they were expected to destroy, and which were thought to threaten the landing beaches, were only 75mm. field guns which were primarily for defence against tank attack from directly in front. Two of the guns were rendered useless by firing two shells through the barrels, but the others were not as effectively disabled[2].

This was to prove to be a mistake, as Otway, not being able to confirm whether his yellow success flare had been spotted, or that the carrier pigeon he released had reached home, retreated from the emplacement rather than risk being shelled by *Aratheusa* if the messages had not been received. In his absence, German gunners from the 736th Grenadier Regiment re-occupied the battery, and later two of the guns were in action against the landing troops. British commandos captured the bunker, but it was to change occupants twice again. A costly exercise for little reward.

---

1 Some accounts state capture as 4.30 am, others record the beginning of the action as 4.35 and lasting 15 minutes. The weight of evidence favours the latter, but in the end, it doesn't really matter.

2 There are conflicting reports as to the number of guns destroyed and how. Whether two or three, the number or method of disabling them did not effect the outcome.

Parachuting into disaster

The main road from Cherbourg to Paris, the N13, passes through the towns of Carentan and Ste Mere Eglise. For the Allies to open up a route from Cherbourg, which they intended to attack from the landward side, the two towns had to be captured. This, probably more than any other operation on the day, resulted in a large waste of human life, not solely from direct enemy action, but from the combination of weather, innaccurate navigation in trying circumstances, and the weight of equipment each man had to carry.

In the late hours of the 5th of June, and well into the 6th, a total of more than 9,200 aircraft, C47s with their paratrooper cargoes, and the gliders they towed, transported 17,000 American parachutists and their equipment – jeeps, field guns, mortars, ammunition and other supplies, in to the drop zones. They were preceded by 120 pathfinders who were to mark specific areas within a fifty square mile area between Carentan and the Merderet, in a rough rectangle behind *Utah Beach*.

Although they jumped, close to the ground, at times from as low as 350 feet, the pathfinders were hopelessly scattered by the unpredictable wind. With less than one third landing accurately, the majority of markers were placed in the wrong places, but with the incoming aircraft experiencing the same problems, and finding it difficult or impossible to spot their particular pathfinder signals, the lack of accuracy was not as important a factor as it may otherwise have been.

Sweeping in from the west, over the coast below Cherbourg, the first waves of gliders and aircraft carrying the paratroopers of the 82nd and 101st Airborne curved left, eastward across the Contentin Peninsula towards their drop zones each side of the Merderet River, a short distance from Ste Mere Eglise, and near Ste Marie du Mont.

Both the US 82nd and 101st Airborne were to parachute in shortly after 1.30 am, and from their landing points they were to approach the towns from the south. The defenders had inundated low lying fields between Highway 13 and the sand dunes, and the only exit off *Utah Beach* was via five causeways, all of which were heavily defended.

Moving through to occupy the small bridges which spanned low lying ground near the Merderet, and between the main towns, the villages, and the sea, the paratroopers' job was to create a clear path for troops and equipment travelling inland from the landing beaches in the north. At least, this was what the intricate plan intended.

Approaching, the C47 pilots became disoriented by flak and the dense low cloud which now covered the areas, and in taking evasive action, navigators lost their bearings. Many gliders either cast off too early or too late, and most became lost in the cloud. Without power to climb or manoeuvre, they were committed to landing within a short distance of cast off, coming down in fields far from the areas with which they had become familiar in course of training. Some crashed into buildings or walls, others broke in half, smashed on the steel triangles, were ripped by wires or impaled on *Rommel's Asparagus*. Others sank into the inundated pasture land.

Paratroopers jumped over what was thought to be solid ground, but which was actually grass growing through swamps which had been flooded. Weighted down by packs and equipment of 70 to 80 pounds (32 to 36 kg), hundreds sank into the mire and quietly drowned. Others, landing safely, subsequently fell into flooded ditches, creeks or swamps and also drowned. Parachutes floated on the surface; attached to the end of each, a body or urgently needed materials.

The 101st's 6,500 paratroopers were distributed along a 25 mile (40 km) path. Most of the survivors did not know where they were. Children's toy frog clickers had been issued with kit, and to the signal of one click, the response was two. Gradually, the clicking frogs assembled in small bands, and attempted to feel their way to their objectives over a landscape which was completely foreign, and in darkness.

One group of approximately one hundred, landed on the wrong side of the Merderet, in the swamps near Moitiers-en Bauptois. Between them and Ste Mere Eglise was 8 miles (13 km), of mostly flooded country, spanned by bridges strongly held by the Germans. Local inhabitants, risking certain execution if caught, spent all night ferrying the Americans in punts they had kept hidden through four years of German occupation.

At the end of the day, losses were estimated as one-third personnel and two-thirds equipment. Even much of the equipment which was located could not be salvaged, as it is an impossible task to extract a jeep, anti tank gun, or even ammunition pack from a swamp, when firm ground may be half a mile (.8 km) away, and with risk of detection and attack constantly looming.

Approaching the town of Ste Mere Eglise, General Gavin's 82nd waited to jump. Six hundred feet below, water glistened in the moonlight through broken cloud. This had to be the Douve, and swiftly the parachutists left their aircraft. However, they had mistaken the flooded Mederet swamps, 5 miles short of the Douve, and loaded with their packs, landed in the flooded areas.

Wading through the water, lost and seeking the objectives they were assigned, many drowned by falling into holes or deep water, or ran into enemy patrols. Paratroopers, overcarried by their transports, jumped through thin cloud into the sea, and others, luckier, landed on beaches or behind the dunes, some from the 101st being captured by *Strongpoint W5* at the eastern extremity of what was soon to be recorded as *Utah Beach*.

One aircraft discharged its cargo late, and instead of landing in clear fields near Ste Mere Eglise, the paratroopers were caught by the wind, and swept back towards the town. With light from a fire in a house near the town square flickering on the parachutes, the troops floated towards its 12th century church, and Roman milestone in the square, where a bucket brigade of residents, guarded by Germans from a flak unit, were attempting to extinguish the flames.

Slowly, the parachutes drifted down, and looking up, the bucket brigade and guards forgot the burning building, as it became immediately obvious that in the middle of a local emergency,[3] the village was being invaded by paratroopers. This was not one of the many false alarms they had experienced in the past. The Germans fired their rifles and Schmeissers at the paratroopers, virtually defenceless on the ends of their lines, and many were dead before they hit the ground.

Some were shot immediately they landed, and others, hanging on trees or power wires, were also shot without the option of surrender. Paratroopers, hanging helpless in their harness from trees or power lines were riddled by fire from half a dozen guns. Before a paratrooper could get to his feet to surrender, he was shot . One of the regimental chaplains was captured and executed.

Suspended below his parachute, Private John Steele of the 505th regiment, 82nd Airborne, watched the scene below with horror, then became aware of his own impending predicament as the tower of the church drew closer, and it with the likelihood of a collision. Striking the ridge of the roof, he slid and clattered down the steep incline until arrested by his parachute catching on one of the stone projections which are a feature of the building.

From the tower, the giant bell, originally tolling the fire alarm, continued its mournful sound, and hanging by his shrouds, the wounded Steele watched, playing dead, deafened by the incessant bell, whilst lit by the flickering flames, the battle in the market square raged below.[4]

Although not more than twenty five of the 505th parachute regiment came down in or near the square, in the confusion caused by the fire, the crowd of townspeople, the thunder of aircraft constantly passing overhead

---

3 Comment has been made that the fire was caused by a pathfinder flare.

4 Steele was cut down by the Germans, escaped, and survived the war.

with their lights on, the Germans appeared to panic, and, according to Mayor Alexandre Renard, lost control.

The increasing wave of noise, the roar of flak emplacements opening up as the advancing carpet of aircraft rolled across Normandy, and the pink confetti of the chutes reflected in the firelight as they drifted off elsewhere, contributed to their agitation. Around the town, numbers on the ground were building as the troopers landed, but resulting from the confused jumps, there was no clear definition between the 82nd and 101st, and small parties of men frequently mixed, hoping to find their own main body. Then, at about 2 am, in what was one of the most premature actions of the day, the German flak unit pulled out.

With daylight, all was quiet in the little town. Parachutes littered the ground, blowing softly in the breeze, and in the fields, deserted gliders, many shattered by contact with obstacles or hard landing in the dark, lay at odd angles, some with their noses in hedges or buildings, others poking out of the foliage over the Norman laneways.

After removing snipers from the church bell tower, Ste Mere Eglise was in Allied hands, but the silence was not to last for long. The battery at Azeville, 4 miles (6.5 km) away, received the news, and opened up, ranging in on the houses, shells killing inhabitants who sought shelter in nearby ditches, and wrecking many of the old grey stone houses. The battle was to run until Friday, with heavy loss of life on both sides and amongst the civilian population.

The British and Canadians, dropping to the east, scattering either side of the Caen Canal, fared little better than the 101st and 82nd near Ste Mere Eglise. The 3rd and 5th Parachute Brigade battalions of the British 6th Airborne Division, totalling more than 4,200 men, spread over a large area, victims of the same problems experienced by the Americans – aircraft dodging flak and losing direction, being unable to locate drop zone markers and the weather, gusts of wind scattering parachutes, men and equipment. Some aircraft were hit, and crashed, taking their human cargoes with them.

Again, as with the US drop zones, and later on the beach approaches, water was the initial enemy. Particularly, the flooded fields of the Dives Valley, the swamps and wetlands, flooded on Rommel's orders, turned the 3rd Brigade's introduction to Normandy into a disaster.

Many of the British paratroopers carried more than 125 lb (57 kg) of equipment, and instantly sank into the criss-crossing mud and water filled ditches, some up to eight feet (2.4 m) deep. Weighed down by their packs, now waterlogged and weighing much more than when dry, even those who fell on to reasonably solid ground had but a slim chance of extricating themselves from the trap.

While individuals struggled to obtain their bearings, or even survive, over the Norman fields floated the sound of an English hunting horn. From the countryside others answered, some close, some faintly far away, their throaty, drifting notes rallying men to begin their tasks of assisting Major Howard's group to hold the bridge at Benouville, and securing the town of Ranville, through which the road to the bridge over the Orne passed. They had also a tight schedule to complete, in clearing a selected obstacle-littered and mined field, so the massive Hamilcar gliders, laden with tanks, anti-tank weapons and ammunition, could safely land.

Ordeal at sea

Mid Channel, the invasion force had peeled off from the assembly area and, following assigned lanes, headed for their discharge points. Beginning with Force U at 2 am, and followed by Force O at 3 am, the transporting vessels lowered their landing craft between 10 and 12 miles (16 to 19 km) offshore, to avoid possible damage from enemy shore batteries.

Launching small craft in the wild weather was a perilous operation, and many of the vessels did not live long in the waves. Men drowned, weighed down by their gear, others were rescued. The surviving landing craft were saved by the jettisoning of equipment and frantic baling by the occupants, using buckets, tins, their steel helmets – anything. At least 10 of the 190 craft sank, and the remainder just stayed afloat.

The wild weather had confined both the Cherbourg and Le Havre E Boat flotillas to port, and normal patrols had not gone out that evening. In the early hours of the morning, in Boulogne, Capt Lt Fimmen of the 4th S Boat Flotilla was woken with news of activity in the Channel. His boats were in readiness, and as they began to leave the harbour, waves of bombers appeared, plastering the port and its facilities with high explosive, forcing Fimmen's boats to retreat to the safety of their bunkers.

In Le Havre, commander of the 5th E Boat Flotilla, Heinrich Hoffmann, received news of activity in the Channel and decided to investigate. With three of his Moewe class boats, Hoffmann left the harbour at 3.30 am and an hour later encountered the smoke screen which had been laid around most of the invasion fleet. Bursting through, the boats emerged to be confronted by the entire fleet, battleships, cruisers and other warships, transports and their escorts, all heading towards Normandy.

Hoffmann swept in to attack, and came under fire from *Warspite* and *Ramillies*, with the three boats firing a total of eighteen torpedoes before retiring into the smoke. All but one missed, that single torpedo striking the Norwegian destroyer *Svenner* in the boiler, breaking her in halves. Heading for Le Havre, Hoffmann attempted to raise the alarm, but his radio had been damaged and the message was not received.[5]

During the entire period of the invasion, all German torpedo boats were confined to their bunkers. They knew the Allies had virtual mastery

---

5 Accounts of the E Boat attack vary, one mentioning the involvement of German armed trawlers, and the firing of torpedoes from behind the smokescreen, but weight of evidence supports the firing in front of the smoke, and only the E Boats being present.

of the skies, and considering the wall of fire they would encounter from the fleet, to venture out would be suicide.

As with the paratroopers' experience on shore, at sea, the weight of personal equipment caused many deaths. Men were weighed down with their tools of trade as well as their rifles and ammunition. Signallers carried cables and radios, infantry carried shovels, first aid kits, additional ammunition, blankets, rations, all of which restricted their mobility, and made boarding a small vessel rising and falling in the sea by as much as 12 feet (3.7 m), extremely hazardous. There were troops who misjudged the leap and either fell from a height, fracturing limbs, or were crushed between the sides of the craft, and others who missed completely and disappeared. Boats lowered from davits were effected by jamming falls, being hit by waves and thrown into the air, slammed against the parent vessel's side or through being incorrectly slipped, either spilling men into the sea, or becoming swamped.

Those on the vessels were anxious, seasick, cold and miserable, and now exhausted from their constant efforts in keeping their craft afloat, were in far less than peak condition for an effective assault on a well defended coast. As dawn approached, aircraft laying smoke flew parallel with the beach, hiding the fleet from visual detection, and although this had no effect upon enemy radar, there was no evidence, even after ships had reached their assigned positions, that they had been spotted.

At 3 am, the *Omaha* armour, the swimming tanks, were launched and almost immediately this operation became a disaster. In the waves, 3.5 miles (5.6 km) off the coast, flotation skirts soon tore, struts twisted and engines flooded. As the ungainly craft wallowed and their crews struggled desperately to keep them afloat, many succumbed to the overwhelming forces of wind and water, and sank with their crews trapped inside. Most of the men who could escape, died on the surface. One compassionate attempt at rescue was forestalled by a marshal's launch heading off the would be rescuer, because orders issued to assault craft were to land their cargoes, not stop to collect survivors. So coxwains looked the other way as their vessels passed through the bobbing lines of living and dead.

A total of 64 tanks was to be launched in two batches, but learning from the experience of the initial 32, of which only five survived – two successfully swimming ashore, and three being unable to leave their transport at the same time as the others – commanders made decisions to close the shore and launch the balance where time in the water was not as long, the waves not as high, and traffic not as intense.

Tanks destined for the British and Canadian sectors fared much better. At 6.30 am the location for launching the *Sword Beach* floating tanks was shortened to 2.8 miles (4.5 km) offshore, and the operation began, with LCTs lowering their ramps and armour trundling down into the sea. All but three of the 40 began the run in. Propellers kicking up the water behind, they headed for the shore in an orderly manner. On the two other British and Canadian beaches, coxwains chose to take their craft close inshore before floating off the tanks.

This is London calling: I bring you an urgent instruction from the Supreme Commander, particularly adressed to all who live within 35 kilometres of any part of the coast. Leave your towns at once. Inform any neighbours who may not be aware of the warning, stay off frequented roads, go on foot and take nothing with you which you cannot easily carry, get as quickly as you can into the open country, do not gather in large groups, as you may be mistaken for troops . . . this first official indication that the invasion was soon to occur, was addressed to French civilians in coastal towns. Many did not observe the advice, preferring to stay in their homes.

Earlier, in an intensified and more locally directed campaign, the 1,100 Bomber Command aircraft had unloaded 5,800 tons of bombs on defences. Now, along the coastline, having no reason for concealment of their objectives or necessity for diversion, both heavy and fighter bombers concentrated on softening the defences. At 5am, Bomber Command's

Lancasters resumed their work over the British-Canadian beaches, and from 5.50 am, the US 8th Air Force systematically bombed defences along the *Utah-Omaha* sector, joining with the Navy in attacking German shore defences in that half-hour before the first landings.

As the landing craft, an assortment of vessels in lines stretching to the horizon, approached the coast, many waterlogged, some damaged and operating with makeshift repairs, the Naval barrage began. It was 5.50 am, and from the throats of scores of guns, large and small, came a roar which reverberated along the coast, a roar pounding off the water and cliff faces, a sound which seconds later was intensified as shells exploded on shore, churning up the soil, smashing concrete. A mighty overwhelming thunder, which to most of the defenders was the first confirmation that this was actually the long awaited invasion – and in Normandy, not Pas-de-Calais.

This was also the day for which the crews of warships had waited, as their guns pounded their targets with the accuracy for which naval gunners are renowned. Trained to hit moving targets from their own moving ships, targets on this occasion were stationary, and for the most part, so were they, and gunnery officers made the most of it. HMS *Belfast's* task was to eliminate the battery at Ver sur Mer, HMS *Emerald*, the battery at Arromanches. USS *Arkansas* prepared the ground for the Omaha landing, *Nevada's* target was Azeville, and USS *Tuscaloosa's* 5 and 8 inch shells exploded in the Ozeville battery.

The emplacements at Pointe du Hoc, soon to be assaulted by US Rangers climbing the cliffs, were shelled by the 14 inch guns of USS *Texas*, having already received attention from Douglas A20 bombers in previous days. HMS *Warspite's* 15 inch guns targeted the battery at Villerville, and HMS *Ajax*, off Arromanches, engaged the Longues battery, situated towards Port en Bessin.

Along the coastline of the Bay of the Seine, the rolling roar continued for half an hour, switching off five minutes before the scheduled first landings, an eerie silence descending, through which the rumble of a thousand engines grew louder as the swarms of landing craft approached their beaches.

First to land were to be the Engineers, and none of them had any illusions as to their chances of survival. Even with protective clothing, they faced the hazards of disarming explosive devices, clearing obstacles and being fired upon without having the time or opportunity to fire back. First landing had been at 4.30 am on the Iles St Marcouf, 3.5 miles (5.6 km) off *Utah Beach*, opposite Ravenoville, and within view of St Marcouf and the shore. Here, in a fruitless exercise, for there were no guns on the barren, uninhabited islands, the demolition party was caught in a maze of explosive devices, immediately losing 20 of their number to mines and booby traps.

Two hours later, on the landing beaches, the engineers' duty was to clear a path for the first waves of landing craft and the assault troops, and it had to be done swiftly. Working against time and often in difficult conditions, under fire and in murky water, the casualty rate was high.

On *Utah*, eight naval diver/engineer squads had to clear a 50 yard gap. Carrying their own explosive demolition charges, each man worked systematically, ignoring the patter and whine of bullets, concentrating on blowing the beach obstacles apart.

On the British and Canadian beaches of *Gold* and *Juno*, wind had forced the tide in ahead of schedule, and some of the mined obstacles were submerged. Naval frogmen went about their task, gradually clearing a narrow path shorewards, disarming mines and clearing the shells which were mounted atop posts, positioned to blow the bottom out of any incoming vessel.

On *Gold*, they removed more than 2,500 hazards, suffering a surprisingly low incidence of casualties, with two killed and ten wounded. On *Omaha Beach*, so intense was the fire, that the engineers, scattered, and more than half arriving late, were forced to abandon their system plan and work ad-hoc, clearing the nearest obstacle. In the time, they cleared one-third of the area intended before the first waves of infantry arrived.

New arrivals severely handicapped the engineers' progress by getting in the way, sheltering alongside obstacles on which they had set demolition charges, and running them over as they crouched down to set their explosives. German gunners paid particular attention to the engineers, and frequently detonated the engineers' charges by gunfire as they were being set. In at least two areas, mine clearing parties arrived without the protection of covering fire. Wading ashore laden with gear, they were shot almost at will by the defenders. On *Omaha*, the engineer casualties were more than 40%.

United States' Beaches

Utah

Touchdown at *Utah Beach* was scheduled for 6.30 am and accomplished dead on time, the first French beach to receive the liberating troops. In contrast with the landings yet to come, this was almost a routine exercise, with light defence from the few emplacements spread between Quineville and the seafront Dunes de Varreville, and at la Madeleine, occupied by *Strongpoint W5*.

W5 had been one of the better equipped seafront defences, with five light artillery pieces ranging from 50 to 88 mm, and assorted automatic weapons housed in concrete, with armoured cupolas as additional protection. The emplacement's function was to stop invaders at the water's edge, holding them there, and acting as spotter for the larger guns at St Martin de Varreville, out of sight close behind the shore defences.

But a particularly effective bombing and naval assault had wrecked the emplacement, fractured telephone wires, and most of the guns were either damaged or buried under sand. There was no longer communication with the main battery, and no support fire. With only the batteries at Crisbecq (St Marcouf) and Azeville remaining operational for any length of time, defences at this point were particularly thin.

As the landing craft approached the shore, the naval bombardment lifted, the successfully launched amphibious tanks fired from the shallows, outside the range of accurate fire from *W5*. Incoming troops raced up the beach, and faced with a seemingly endless fleet steaming offshore, and promising more to come, the already stunned defenders were either captured or retreated, allowing engineers to clear obstacles almost unhindered. Within two hours, the beach was completely open.

Mostly, this was the fortunate result of incorrect navigation, with the small vessels being carried a mile to the south-east by tide and wind, and landing at one of the more lightly defended sections. This also placed them further from the big guns of Azeville and St Marcouf. As occurred during the Canadian landing at *Juno*, an escort boat was caught by the tide, and missing the planned landing area opposite exits three and four, came in near Utah's extreme eastern boundary.

The planned link-up with the paratroopers and glider borne troops would have to be made by an angled drive to the south west, which also provided the advantage of approaching the beach defences in a flanking movement on their vulnerable landward sides. Few, if any, of the defences could handle an assault from the south, for the concrete emplacements faced the sea. In some instances they were sensibly bypassed completely, for if someone can't shoot at you, it's better to take care of those who can.

The combination of landing at low tide on the flat beaches beyond the range of accurate small arms fire, at the wrong place, where the defences had been severely mauled from the air and, lacking communications, could not call in artillery, was certainly a stroke of good fortune.

The advance contingent of engineers, still suffering casualties, cleared a path through the beach obstacles and moved to the retaining wall which separated the dunes and low lying country from the sea. This was now an obstacle, forming a barrier between beach and the country beyond, and to gain access, had to be broached. Using bangalore torpedoes, engineers cleared concrete and wire obstacles, opening exit channels along the beachfront.

Soon, armor had moved into the dunes and was attacking concrete emplacements. Tanks, unmolested except for bullets clanging harmlessly off their casings, deliberately moved into position, lining up their targets with care, and firing at will. Behind them, the second wave marines were moving in, following the original 600, while support equipment – trucks, bulldozers, jeeps, weapons, ammunition and more armour – was landed in a steady stream with minimal losses, even though encountering artillery fire as inland batteries found their range.

Losses occurred, with 197 casualties of which 60 had drowned, but by evening 22,000 men and 1,800 vehicles had landed.

USS *Corry*, anchored off Utah, was the marines' artillery. Firing nonstop, the destroyer had maintained a constant barrage, raining 5 inch shells on any emplacement which threatened the landing, and by doing so, herself became a target to be eliminated by the shore defences.

Sited near the village of St Marcouf, the 210 mm guns of Crisbeq battery had been slogging it out with the battleship USS *Nevada* since first light. *Nevada's* primary target was the Azeville battery, only a few kilometres south west of St Marcouf, but now, Crisbeq turned its attention upon *Corry*, which was now weaving to avoid the battery's particularly accurate fire.

Hampered by offshore reefs, the vessel struggled at reduced speed to manoeuvre and at the same time place as much distance between her stern and Crisbeq as possible. In the hands of Lieutenant Commander George Hoffman, *Corry* headed seawards, building up speed, the battery's shells exploding in her wake, escape almost achieved. It was then she ran into a mine.

Split along bottom and sides, with momentum carrying her half a mile further before the deck and superstructure, which had been holding the vessel together, buckled, *Corry* sank, bow and stern pointing skywards in a defiant V. The Crisbeq guns then scored hit after hit, detonating the ship's magazine but wasting their own ammunition, for even though the ensign flew from the masthead protruding above the sea, *Corry* had become the second Allied destroyer to be lost on D-Day.

Troops and armor, using roads and the bridges, moved inland to join the airborne forces. Amphibious craft waded through the flooded lowlands which the Germans had inundated by simply concreting over the mouths of drainage streams which flowed into the sea. By early evening they were in a position to establish the first US command post in France, in the town of Audoville La Hubert, at the Buisson farm on the outskirts of the village.

Omaha

Omaha Beach extends from Pointe et Raz de la Percee to Ste Honorine, and is slightly curved, with the main defensive emplacements in the hills on either side, covering the beach exit to Colleville, and also the massive fortifications of Pointe du Hoc to the West. As the landing craft approached, a combination of tide, wind, and the land being obscured by smoke, caused them to arrive east of the planned zone, in territory with which they were not familiar through briefings, and generally less suitable for an assault. Distributed in a line of up to a mile from the correct location, and surfing shorewards, craft broached, spilling their cargoes. Some, swerving out of control, struck and holed each other, hit mines or ripped their bottoms out on submerged obstacles. It was a shambles. Then the artillery, mortars and small arms struck.

Bombing had failed to destroy the defences, in fact much of the weight of bombs did not strike the intended targets at all. The beaches, where it was expected that bomb craters would provide shelter, were unscarred. Shelling had caused considerable damage to the open emplacements but not markedly effected the firepower which now lashed the craft and troops below.

Men floundering in the water, having been tipped out of their landing craft, or jumping as their vessels were hit, were machine gunned or drowned by the weight of their equipment. The swimming tanks which were to provide support had not arrived, and the rocket firing barges were being held out of range by superior German artillery. Worse, when the barges fired their rockets, they landed short, on the beach, effectively preventing any advance, even had the men been able to do so. When the two surviving tanks from the initial disastrous launch arrived, they were put out of action by German artillery. Landing craft containing heavy weapons and ammunition had been shelled and were on fire. Of 13 bulldozers, a scant 3 survived.

The infantrymen were on their own.

From their emplacements, machine guns cut the Americans down as they emerged from the landing craft. The 105 mm howitzers at Houtteville ranged in, spraying shrapnel and sand as their shells exploded amongst the troops huddling in or behind whatever meagre shelter the beach could provide. *Dog Green* and *Fox Green* were the worst. *Dog Green*, was a 1,000 yard (914 m) stretch of beach in front of Colleville and Vierville, and again, infantry arrived without the planned backup, to a reception showing little effect of the previous Allied bombardment.

The first wave of large landing craft encountered artillery fire, and one-third sank. The survivors were stopped at the first sandbar, dropped their ramps, and the troops, wading ashore through the channel, ran into a wall of machine gun fire. Some, observing bullets frothing the water through which they would have to wade, went over the sides and, hampered by their gear, attempted to swim underwater. Those not hit or drowned, eventually lay in the shallows, sheltering behind the bodies of their dead comrades, inching forward with the tide, otherwise unable to move[6].

Here, less than one-third survived. One company of 75 was reduced to 12. Of two Ranger companies totalling 130, only 65 survived. Loss of equipment was enormous. One section lost three quarters of its machine guns, and three quarters of their communications equipment. All along *Omaha*, the same disaster was occurring. Minefields had not been cleared, so what armour had arrived, was trapped.

Wet, weakened by the effects of seasickness, young and terrified, having lost much of their equipment, GIs lay in the shallows, inching up with the tide, or, crouched on a narrow strip of unfriendly beach, the few lucky ones huddled against rocks, praying for survival.

The plan was for succeeding waves of troops to land, and soon the second wave was arriving on schedule, to the same reception. Shells and mortars struck landing craft, killing the occupants. The tide was rising at 7 feet (2 m) an hour, and submerging the live obstacles. Men were killed as they came down ramps or waded ashore. Deaths in the water equalled those on the beach. The second wave was closely followed by a third and fourth, and in the open, with men and equipment jam-packed along a swiftly narrowing strip, with bodies and equipment littering the waterline, and no prospect of opening up an exit from the beach, *Omaha* was a total picture of confusion and doubt.

It required one incident to turn around the deteriorating situation, and

---

[6] Accounts of the height of the water vary, some describing the tide as being low and on the turn, with wounded drowning in a few inches of water. Others claim the obstacles were almost submerged, being struck by landing craft as they approached. There is no doubt that both incidents, and others occurred, and the tide certainly was low, but in the lesser sheltered areas, wind may have forced the water further up the beach, creating a false tide. As the landing area extended for over a mile, conflicting eyewitness accounts are both probably correct for the area of observation.

88   Footsteps of D-Day

that incident was an officer who said *are you going to lay there and get killed, or do something about it?* (or alternatively, *there are only two kinds of men who will be on this beach – those who are dead, and those who are about to be killed*, depending on the report).

Spurred into movement, on *Dog White*, action was taken to blow the barbed wire defences, and the troops streamed through, dodging minefields from which the now rapidly retreating Germans had failed to remove warning signs. But in the other sectors, the situation was precarious. Constant machine gunning, mortars and artillery fire pounded the beaches, and for those able to get off the sand, mines laid in the dunes, some fitted with trip wires, others which sprang into the air before detonating, took their toll.

For Rommel loved mines. During previous coastal inspections, he appeared totally preoccupied with devising methods of laying additional mines, seeing sand dunes or pasture in terms of capacity to accommodate a quantity of these devices. Gradually the defences were worn down by the constant weight of the forces arriving, but in many instances, the advance was literally over the bodies of those who had triggered the mines. As the US troops began to move inland, they were supported when requested, by naval gunfire from destroyers which swooped inshore, and the rocket barges which were now able to approach and attack.

Pointe Du Hoc

To the north west of *Omaha*, a cliff juts into the sea. With bays on either side, and edged by 30 metre cliffs, it commands the adjacent beaches, and is the perfect site for a battery, particularly one for defence of the beach to the right, a stretch of sand and shingle, soon to have a permanent place on maps as *Omaha*, and in history books as "Bloody Omaha".

The plan was for more than 200 men of the 2nd US Ranger Battalion to climb the cliffs at 6.30 am to capture the network of emplacements, and more particularly the artillery. For climbing, they assembled an assortment of equipment ranging from the more conventional rock climbing gear and cartridge fired grappling hooks, to ladders borrowed from the London Fire Brigade. The 13 landing craft were escorted by a pilot which initially mistook Pointe de la Percee for Pointe du Hoc, and time taken rectifying this error placed their boats on the beach half an hour late. In this time, the defenders had managed to regroup after the bombardment, and despite fire from the destroyer *Satterlee*, inshore backup for the battleship USS *Texas*, they were lining clifftops ready to deal with the incoming Rangers.

Four of the landing craft were either swamped or sunk by enemy gunfire, the remaining nine beaching close under the cliffs from which the defenders threw grenades, fired automatic weapons, dislodged grappling hooks, or cut the ropes which the Rangers were climbing. It was almost an assault on a castle from another age.

Suffering heavy losses, most had climbed the cliff by 7.30 am, and then set about rooting the Germans out of those tunnels and dugouts which had survived days of aerial assault, and the recent naval bombardment. The ground resembled a moonscape, heavily cratered, littered with concrete rubble and slabs from which the expected heavy guns were absent. These were eventually found near a roadway to the rear of their intended site, complete with ammunition, and undamaged. A party of Rangers soon disabled them and returned to help the others in removing all resistance.

At the end of the action, 135 of the original 225 Rangers were either dead or wounded. Pointe du Hoc was theirs, but the guns they feared were not installed, and could not have been brought into action quickly enough to threaten the *Omaha* landing.

British and Canadian Beaches

Under cover of the same heavy naval barrage which protected the US troops in the run-up to the scheduled 6.30 am landings at *Utah* and *Omaha*,

British and Canadian forces had approached their beaches from Port en Bessin to Ouistreham. Schedules ranged up to 8 am, with the first roll-off occurring at 7.25 am on *Gold Beach*, between Port en Bessin and La Riviere.

Gold

Here, armour was the first to arrive, sheltering the infantry, a surprise for the defenders who had not expected tanks from the 8th British Armoured Brigade to be firing on them from 800 yards (730 m) away. These had been unloaded at the beach instead of being expected to swim ashore as originally intended, and no losses had been experienced. The pre-assault bombardment had been particularly successful, and apart from a few scattered field pieces, the Germans had little more than machine guns, a few mortars, and their small arms with which to oppose the advance. At La Riviere, so demoralised were the defenders, that British infantry landed almost unopposed, although pockets of resistance were encountered from isolated sections which had escaped the bombardment, particularly around Le Hamel.

But it was not a simple task for most. Landing craft, caught by waves, broached, and out of control, struck mined obstacles and the steel triangles, resulting in many casualties. The 1st Hampshires, coming in on the western sector, ran into a wall of fire from mortars and machine guns.

Pathfinder engineers fulfilled the vital role of clearing an entrance through the mined obstacles, particularly *Element C* the spiked mesh, mined to either rip or fracture the bottom of any craft with which it came in contact. Working mostly underwater on a rising tide, and in murky conditions, frogmen proceeded to disarm each obstacle and flatten the panels.

In contrast, the Ist Dorsets took little more than half an hour to clear the beach, and the Green Howards took only a fraction longer to achieve their objectives. The Dorsets' AVRE armour swiftly dealt with whatever opposition remained, Crab and Bobbin tanks cleared mined fields, covered soft sand patches and worked quickly behind the defences, heading for Arromanches, site of the future artificial harbour.

Tanks, firing from the water's edge, worked on the still live areas of the German 716th Division. In one instance, the Russian conscripts deserted, leaving only their German officers and NCOs to resist the incoming forces.

One Victoria Cross was awarded on D-Day – to Sgt Major Stanley Hollis, who in a drive to capture the Mont Fleury battery, single handed, and in the face of machine gun fire, put out of action a German pillbox and later an enemy field gun after a running battle. This action, in which he constantly came under intense fire, cleared the exit from the eastern end of *Gold*. Hollis' total for the day was 12 killed and 20 prisoners .

Col Phillips' No. 47 Royal Marine Commando's task was to swing left and capture Port en Bessin from the rear, then join up with the US forces coming off *Omaha*. Port en Bessin snuggles in a valley, the channel between the hills opening out into a bay flanked by cliffs. Attack from the sea would be costly, and even if the incoming vessels gained the entrance, chances were they would be sunk and jam the basin, thus defeating the intent of capturing a clear port.

The objective had to be tackled from the landward side, and 47 Commando, after a 10 mile (16 km) hike, each man loaded down with 80 pounds (36 kg) of equipment, had the job of doing this. Fierce fire in the landing area forced a diversion, then underwater obstacles, mines and the surf took their toll. Many of the commandos drowned, and most of those who were able to free themselves from the packs and reach the sand, were now unarmed and without their specialist equipment.

One third of the landing craft failed to reach shore, and one third of the force was now without arms. Rushing off the beach, they executed a whirlwind assault on La Rosiere, capturing weapons to arm those who had lost their guns, pressing on to Port en Bessin, where two miles from their objective, they camped for the night, ready to call in the naval bombardment next morning.

By early evening, the troops from *Gold Beach* had joined the Canadians off *Juno*, but would take longer to make contact with the *Omaha* forces.

Sword

Also at 7.30 am, the first of the 3rd British Infantry Division's landing craft scraped on to the shingle between Ouistreham and Lion sur Mer. Pre-invasion briefings had identified *Sword* as being the most likely area to produce severe casualties, and levels of up to 80% were forecast. But the result was nowhere near the extent predicted, and possibly this relief caused the actual level of resistance to appear minimal.

Defences in this condensed three mile beach had been severely damaged by an accurate and sustained two hour naval bombardment, supplemented by fighter bomber attacks which followed an also accurate bombing by Liberators in the early hours of the morning. The few remaining guns had difficulty locating targets, which were obscured by smoke and haze drifting across their lines of vision from surrounding on-shore fires.

The swimming tanks, launched two and a quarter miles offshore, suffered 50% casualties from swamping and collisions, but the half that did reach the water's edge, arriving five minutes after the infantry, remained in the surf with only their turrets showing, presenting small and indistinct targets. From this hull down in the water position, they were able sit and pick off areas of resistance on shore with minimal risk. A few were swamped by waves or damaged by shellfire, but the main body was able to proceed ashore behind the AVRE flails, bulldozers, and the beach clearing teams.

Even with defences reduced by an effective bombardment, troops still ran into machine gun and small arms fire, the 2nd East Yorkshire regiment suffering heavy casualties. One hour after landing, two of the three planned exits had been opened, the vehicles and machinery pouring through. Although some minefields were still active, most had been destroyed by the pre-invasion action and posed little threat.

In isolated areas, the defenders regrouped and attacked. The German 736th Grenadier Regiment fought back, following the shoreline from Riva Bella, almost to Lion sur Mer, where weight of opposition eventually overwhelmed them. Along the coast, those emplacements remaining were virtually under seige, unable to defend themselves from the rear, with the enemy on their roofs using flame throwers or pitching grenades through apertures. Reinforced by Brigadier Lord Lovat's 1st Special Service Brigade, which was to open up Ouistreham and relieve Major Howard's small group at Ranville, forces fanned out behind the beachhead, and by 10.00 am were headed inland.

Reliable accounts of the *Sword* landing differ considerably. Again, this is probably the result of personal experience, depending upon where the individual was at the time, heightened by some measure of relief where opposition was not particularly strong. From reports of heavy casualties, with bodies piled on the beach, the picture varies to one of being described as "just like a training run", an opinion which the 2nd Yorkshires would probably dispute. For them, fierce resistance from Lion sur Mer and isolated pockets resulted in heavy casualties, and their losses contrasted with other sections where it is recorded, a holiday atmosphere brought the local citizenry down to the beaches to greet the troops with embraces, and in some instances, champagne.

Juno

The Canadian 3rd Division was the last scheduled to touch down on their allotted beach, code named *Juno*. This later time was necessary as reefs in the landing area were exposed at low water, and while waiting for them to become covered, the running tide had carried the Canadian fleet too far east, where it came under heavy fire. Weaving back to the correct position, against tide, waves and wind, placed them half an hour late, and in this period anti-invasion obstacles were swiftly being covered by the rising water. Requiring the tide to cover the reefs for clearance, water would also cover iron triangles and mined defences, placing the Canadians in a no-win situation. Breakers and a confused sea chop around the reefs produced heavier seas than were experienced on other beaches, adding to their difficulties.

For the *Juno* contingent, St Aubin sur Mer was the trouble spot. Two landing craft struck submerged objects and sank. The commandos they carried drowned in yet another instance of lives wasted, as weight of equipment, waterlogged clothing and heavy boots dragged men down without any hope of escape. Defences at *Juno* had been less affected than elsewhere by the bombardment and poured out a steady stream of fire.

Men were hit as they waded ashore, and more landing craft came to grief. With mined obstacles quickly submerging, engineers were unable to render them safe. The D-D (swimming) tanks were launched as close to shore as possible, almost on top of the rapidly covering mines. Two were damaged, but the remainder engaged the defences, particularly those established either side of the Suells.

At both Courseulles and Berniers, strong opposition from the untouched defences caused casualties and delays, with some areas not being captured until the next day. In many instances, although they wore German uniforms, many of the defenders were Russian or Polish prisoners pressed into German military service, and only too willing to surrender. Some Germans even volunteered to cease fighting and thus improve their prospects for surviving the war.

As more armour rolled ashore, troops and heavy weapons following, opposition flagged, and by 10 am the beach and areas close by were secure. Wastage of shipping in this sector was particularly significant, with many of the large armour transports being damaged or destroyed.

Entering Saint Marcouf, 1944

Much tidier in 1993

96 Watching the rear, Laneway beside the church of St Marcouf, June 1944

From the main road, June 1993

Carentan, June 1944

The angel's wing survived the assault, but not the peace

A US tank crosses the Cherbourg-Paris railway line at Carentan, June 1944

Intersection with the strategic N13 Paris-Cherbourg highway, June 1993

Entering Ste Marie du Mont from the main *Utah Beach* landing point

This road runs from La Madeleine, which housed *Strongpoint W5*

100　Troops off *Utah*. Entering Ste Marie du Mont around the square of The Church of St Mary

Ste Marie du Mont was virtually undamaged

Flotsam of war. Beach at Arromanches following the worst storm for 40 years, June 1944

Arromanches, the seaside holiday town, June 1993

Arromanches. The Mulberry caissons on the beach and at sea, June 1993

Mulberry caissons, Arromanches, June 1993

Arromanches seafront, June 1944

Their excellent museum is to the left of this photograph

General Sir Bernard Montgomery at Port en Bessin, 10th June 1944

Port en Bessin, 10th June 1993

War and peace. Coming ashore, armoured carrier, 1944

Going fishing. "Rubber Duckie", 1993

106   Bottom of the harbour. German flak ship, Port en Bessin, 10th June 1944

Col Phillips' 47 RM Commando entered along this side of the basin. Photo 10th June 1993

Apart from the small landing craft losses on the inward journey, where their coxwains at least had a chance of seeing the obstacles, if not avoiding them, on the return journey most of the mined obstacles were covered and remained armed. In one instance, 24 landing craft set off from the beach and only four reached their depot ships, the majority being mined or ripped apart by the steel triangles which engineers had been prevented by the tide from removing.

From the three beaches, men and machinery streamed inland, each with their own defined objective, whether a link-up with Major Gale's paratroopers at Ranville and Benouville, or, swinging to the right from *Gold*, seeking to meet the first GIs off *Omaha*. Col Phillips' 47 Royal Marine Commando headed for Port en Bessin, where they were to wait on the outskirts, and enter under the following morning's naval barrage.

The German response

Now all five main beaches were occupied by the Allies, but their foothold was tenuous, with extensive consolidation required before any claim for a first day's success could be made.

Despite the many setbacks, it could have been far worse. So successful had been the execution of *Fortitude*, that the German High Command still considered the Normandy operation to be a diversion. They were so convinced that the invasion (*Schwerpunkt*), when it came, would be through Calais, that Hitler, who had taken his usual sleeping tablet at 3.00 am, was allowed to slumber on.

OKW chief of operations, Col Gen Alfred Jodl, appeared to attach little importance to the early morning activities, even though he had received reports from von Runstedt which indicated von Runstedt's own alarm. As late as 6.00 am he was going about his routine duties and even approved the visit of General Walter Warlimont, his deputy, to Italy as the Allied gains in that sector were causing considerable concern.

Hitler had not been informed, and Rommel was in Germany. The atmosphere at headquarters was almost one of apathy, as though this had happened many times previously with no consequences, and was only another of the enemy's eccentric games.

Panzer Lehr

There is a possibility that use of Panzer Lehr could have tipped the balance, or at least delayed the Allies sufficiently for the defenders to bring reserves into battle. Countering their involvement would be the Allies' complete mastery of the air, and the extreme vulnerability of armour and transports to fighter-bomber attack. Nevertheless, involvement of mobile gun platforms carrying 75 mm guns and the deadly 88's, ranging along the comparatively short 60 mile (97 km) length of the landing beaches, could have made the invasion infinitely more difficult.

At their headquarters 80 miles (130 km) south of Paris, Major General Fritz Bayerlin's Panzer Lehr, although on alert, was still far from the action, but Jodl was not prepared to release the tanks without Hitler's permission, and Hitler was still asleep. He was unconvinced that this was an invasion and not willing to take the personal risk of committing the crack armored division on what could prove to be fruitless errand. Consolidating this attitude was a report from *Omaha* that the incoming forces were trapped on the beach, the sand was strewn with bodies and wreckage, and it was only a matter of time before the invaders were pushed back into the sea.

Accurate as it may have been from an individual's viewpoint, this single emotional report from an elated officer did not represent the entire coastal operation, but in the confused atmosphere, and absence of convincing reports to the contrary, the information was seized upon and used in further influencing opinion that the diversionary foray would soon be defeated. Obviously, this was to be another Dieppe, only larger.

A significant factor contributing to the confusion was an absence of accurate reporting from the coast and the unsettling effect of diversionary tactics. With wires either blasted or cut, communications had been disrupted by bombing, and now were being sabotaged by the the French Resistance. There were exceptions, such as St Marcouf, where wires laid loosely in deep open trenches could whip and move with the explosions, and not fracture. Here, communications held throughout the day and in instances were used by the Allies afterwards. But such examples were rare.

Conflicting accounts, whilst perhaps truthful at the time, described the viewer's opinions, and those opinions depended upon an individual situation which could vary considerably. Further adding to the confusion, dummy parachutists, scattered paratroopers landing in unlikely areas, and the unusual radar readings, hampered the forming of a reliable picture and subsequent plan of action.

So Hitler was allowed to sleep on. Panzer Lehr was anchored in position, and even the alert was cancelled. Nothing was to be done without the Führer's order. This inaction was to cost dearly, for as the hours passed, so the opportunity to move diminished, as daylight was fighter-bomber territory.

Near the coast at Benouville, the action of Panzer Grenadiers, using self propelled 75 mm guns, 20 mm on half tracks, and mortars, but lacking tanks, could possibly have turned the *Sword* sector battle in their favour, had that armour been available. But at this stage, although some tanks were on the move, they were too far away to be of assistance. Eighty of the 716th 1st Battalion drove into the paratroopers' areas near the Orne, where Major Howard's men were tenaciously holding their bridge at Benouville, and 37 other tanks were also on the move; those engaged in war games near Falaise were placed on action readiness, and transferred to Lebisey. Then, a total of 95 tanks headed for the sea in what was to be the final significant German attempt to break the D-Day invasion.

Advance infantry units of the 192nd Panzer Grenadier Regiment had already broken through to the coast, luckily emerging in an unoccupied gap between *Juno* and *Sword* beaches, near Luc sur Mer. In probably the only piece of unoccupied ground along the entire coastline, Grenadiers watched the invasion taking place on either side, waiting for their orders, and the tanks. This was a gap unknown to the Allies, and presented a perfect opportunity for the German defenders to drive a wedge between the two beaches and frustrate the planned link-up.

Inland, Col Herman von Oppeln Bronikowski's 21st Panzer tanks were bogged down in the rubble that once was Caen. Unable to advance through the town, Bronikowski was forced to skirt the city, losing valuable time. Spaced 100 yards apart to lessen the impact of fighter bomber attack, the tanks ran through the countryside, fanning out into two groups, one to occupy the high ground of Bieville and the other headed for the nearby hills at Periers. But they had been beaten to it. The British were already in position, where their long range anti-tank guns commanded the surrounding ground.

Bronikowski was out-ranged and out gunned. Inside 10 minutes, 14 precious tanks had been destroyed. With withdrawal their only option, they retreated and dug into defensive positions, hull down in the earth, with only their turrets showing.

This last operation, upon which the hopes of a Normandy counter offensive hung, had been unsuccessful. The 21st Panzer had now become an instrument of defence and eventually, defeat.

In one of the unexplained events of D-Day, the British did not follow up and enter Caen, which, with demoralized German troops streaming inland, was there for the taking. As a direct consequence, the city would not be captured for another six weeks.

At the OKW 10.00 am briefing, the possibility of the disturbance in Normandy being an invasion was discussed, but release of the Panzers was not on the agenda. Field Marshal Rommel, still at home in Germany, received the first reliable news of the Allied landings shortly after 10 am. Obviously this was not a feint, and for the first time in more than nine hours, nine wasted hours, an officer of the German Senior Command took the matter seriously. Rommel's first action was to prepare to return to his command, and at this time, it is unlikely he was aware of the Panzer Lehr hold up.

After a delay of more than eleven hours, permission for the Panzer Lehr and 12th SS Division to move north was received. But now it was mid afternoon, and to begin a movement of men and equipment of this scale, in daylight, which at this time of the year had at least eight hours until dusk, would be to court disaster. Clouds of dust stirred up by the vehicles would be sufficient to attract fighter bombers like bees, and the attacks would destroy Panzer Lehr as an operational force. Even movement at night was not without hazards, as aircraft lit the ground below with flares, turning night into day, blinding the gunners in their vehicles, not that light ground fire was particularly effective against the armoured Typhoons, Mustangs and Spitfires.

Eventually, Panzer Lehr began to move, and orders were given to spread out, travel from shelter to shelter, avoiding clear ground in daylight.

As the perilous journey began, ahead of the columns lay a maze of cratered roads, towns choked with rubble which had to be skirted, rivers to be crossed where bridges had been destroyed, and the inevitable fighter-bombers. Roaming the sky from first light, the aircraft were over France, attacking anything that moved – trucks, locomotives, troop concentrations and tanks – with machine guns, cannons, rockets and bombs.

A huge concentration such as Panzer Lehr could not effectively spread out, and tanks were prime targets. Armored personnel carriers, trucks, even General Bayerlin's staff car, were strafed as the Division fell victim to these almost unstoppable airborne weapon platforms. Of the depleted Luftwaffe there was little sign.

Dark specks on dusty roads, or leaving tracks through corn fields, vehicles could be easily identified from the air. Often hunting in pairs, the fighter-bombers circled at a distance, selected their targets, lined up, and at tree top height came streaking along the roadway, destroying all in their path and impeding further progress with the wreckage and craters they left behind. Two or three runs were possible in one attack, until, ammunition exhausted, the aircraft departed, to be replaced by others attracted by the smoke, whilst the survivors below lay huddled in ditches with what seemed to be the world exploding around them.

Nothing was ignored. Even the solitary despatch rider was fair game, being relentlessly pursued, harried, and eventually shot off his motorcycle. There were unavoidable instances of mistaken identity, with French citizens being caught up in the fighting. One farmer seeking to make use of the situation, seized an abandoned a German truck, possibly hoping to store it in his shed for later use. Unfortunately he made the mistake of driving across country and was immediately pounced upon by a patrolling aircraft.

The nightmare journey of Panzer Lehr was further impeded by the local citizens who removed, obliterated, or repositioned road signs. Although well equipped with navigational aids, it does assist swift progress if the correct signage is in place, even if only to confirm a position. It is inconvenient at best, at worst, it results in confusion and delay. In the case of Panzer Lehr, it caused long lines of vehicles to concertina whilst the leaders debated which turn to take.

Under cover of darkness, the columns entered Argentan, a town now blazing under sustained Allied air attack. In a confusion of blocked streets, dust from rubble and explosions, and blazing debris, vehicles strove to pick their way through the narrow spaces between buildings, while flares lit up the night sky and aircraft circled overhead. Jammed in the inferno, with no clear exit, many vehicles were lost. Those which escaped, and those which had not entered the town, circled beyond the areas of illumination, and heading west, struck out along the cratered roadway to Flers. The night's events had spread the Division, and at dawn, the advance party was at Conde sur Novieau, 28 miles (45 km) south of Caen. The convoy was now spread over a wide area, and a standing order to maintain radio silence did not assist in managing the situation.

With the tanks far behind, being delayed by having to take cover from fighter bomber attacks, attempting to negotiate the blocked streets of towns and bombed out bridges in their path, the convoy's progress was painfully slow. Roadways strewn with blackened, smoking wreckage marked their passing, and massive losses were being taken without having the opportunity to fire a shot. Although not even safe at night, the only possible action which could be taken to preserve the surviving equipment was to hole up in a forest by day, and travel by night, which meant losing valuable time.

So Panzer Lehr's journey proceeded out of D-Day and into the next four days. It would be five days before the Division reached the main battle zone, by which time the Allied forces were well established.

Guns on the hill

The batteries of St Marcouf (Crisbeq) and Azeville provided stubborn and courageous opposition on the 6th of June, and for many days afterwards.

The St Marcouf battery is sited almost 1 mile (1.6 km) from the village of that name, and 1.5 miles (2.4 km) from the sea, on a rise above the hamlet of Crisbeq. Ideally positioned, both concrete casemates (2 of the planned 4), commanded the *Utah* beaches, with a clear view from St Vaast to Grandcamp and of the Iles St Marcouf, 3 miles (5 kilometres) off the coast, within range of the long barrels of the 210 mm naval guns which had been fitted and tested in April.

Crisbeq was a particular example of the disruption Allied bombing had caused to transport and delivery of equipment, as the battery was without armored cupolas for protecting the external AA guns. Also missing were the massive steel shields for the casemate openings. These had been manufactured, but were either delayed, or lying forgotten in a railway junction somewhere inland. Other materials were in short supply, so only two main casemates had been completed, with a control room on the other side of the roadway, and lacking rangefinders for gunnery control, Crisbecq's had been home made.

Crewed by more than 300 older men, mostly Kreigsmarine officers, ratings, and ranks from other services, the battery was well fortified, with mined perimeters and interconnecting concrete lined trenches up to 12 feet (3.6 m), deep. The third concrete control emplacement housed a 150 mm gun.

From April, the battery had been target for a sustained program of low level bombing, which reached a climax on the 5th of June when an estimated total of 600 tons of explosives descended, destroying all six 75 mm AA guns, filling in many of the trenches, wrecking much of the fortification work, detonating the land mines, and ploughing over the ground. Shortly afterwards, the battery came under fire from an American paratroop patrol which had mistaken Crisbeq for St Martin De Varreville, 4 miles (6.5 km) to the east.

The toy clicker frog, found on one captured American, excited curiosity, and then it occurred that the sudden frog activity in the swamp was not frogs at all, but paratroopers moving around, communicating with each other with their clickers for identification. Gathering a patrol, Lance Corporal Albert Muller moved into the darkness, clicking the captured metal frog, scooping in paratrooper after paratrooper, until more than 20 Americans had been bagged. Brought before the battery's commanding officer, Lieutenant Ohmsen, the first example of Allied attention to detail and knowledge of the defences became apparent to the Germans, with the discovery of a map which marked in detail all surrounding features, including gunnery co-ordinates which the Germans themselves did not know. A similar incident was to be repeated in Cherbourg within a fortnight.

From early D-Day, Crisbeq was active in engaging the naval forces, making the situation uncomfortable for troops on *Utah*, and shelling the Iles St Marcouf. German records claim two destroyers sunk by the guns of St Marcouf, but the US lost only one destroyer that day – *Corry*, which struck a mine attempting to avoid Crisbeq's shells and the inshore reefs. There is no doubt *Corry* had been sunk by the time the Crisbeq guns began recording strikes on that portion of the hull still above water.

For almost three hours from first light, the Crisbeq guns maintained their rate of fire, until the first was put out of action by a strike on the front of the casemate. An hour later, USS *Nevada* scored a hit through the aperture of number two gun, a large open area necessary for the barrel's travel which should have been protected by the undelivered armoured plates.

Apart from the naval bombardment, Ohmsen had his problems to the rear. US troops from the *Utah Beach* landings had reached St Marcouf and were being held off by the battery's sole ground defence, a repaired 20 mm AA gun. Outflanking this single weapon, US troops were soon on the roof of the bunker, so Ohmsen called up fire from the nearby Azeville battery, fire which swept the Americans off the roof. Under the impression they were being shelled by their own side, the Americans abandoned equipment in their haste to retreat.

Recovering the US weapons, repairing their own machine guns, and one of the 210 mm guns, the men of Crisbeq, with reinforcements, would fight on for another five days until in a hopeless situation, Ohmsen completed a brilliantly executed retreat. Under cover darkness, on the 11th of June, he led the surviving 56 men on a 6 mile (9.5 km) trek to the

German lines, leaving 21 of the more seriously wounded, and the medical officer behind.

To the Battle of Normandy

When night came over the Normandy beaches, and mists began to rise from the low country behind, there came almost to an end what was described by Field Marshal Erwin Rommel, as "The longest day".

If there is a visible dividing line, it probably comes with nightfall, although fighting continues on a lesser scale. With the arrival of dawn on the 7th of June, the Battle of Normandy began, a savage and bloody conflict which was to continue until August the 22nd with the virtual annihilation of the German 5th Armoured Army and 7th Army in what is known as the *Falaise Pocket*.

In this area, 19 miles (30 km) long and half as wide, in a loop running westwards from Chambois almost to Argentan, north to Necy and back through Trun, more than 100,000 men and their equipment were trapped under constant fighter-bomber, artillery, armoured, and infantry attack.

They had nowhere to go, as the Allies squeezed the neck shut from Chambois upward, and from Champosoult downward. Some slipped through a gap at Coudehard, including Lt General Freiherr von Lüttwitz's 2nd Panzer Division's remaining fifteen tanks, which plunged through a gap between Chambois and Trun, a gap forced by the 116th Panzer Division, which extracted many of their own vehicles in the process.

On Tuesday, August the 22nd, Canadian troops of the 3rd Infantry Division captured Tournai.

At 8 am that morning, the guns in Normandy fell silent, and the process of recovery began.

CHAPTER FIVE

THE TOWNS

In any military action, the suffering of a population takes many forms. Death or injury, illness, hunger, loss of housing, lack of clothing, exposure to the cold and complete disruption of their lives are the principal hazards these innocent bystanders face. No matter how carefully planned, an operation always runs a high risk of incurring civilian casualties, either because they live in or near a strategic target, or because they just get in the way. In Normandy, homes, and even entire towns were destroyed, the inhabitants became casualties, and often this occurred long before the actual landings.

Aircraft mistook landmarks and unloaded bombs on peaceful villages, and the pre-invasion softening up process caused death and damage. Where the Germans were still in occupation, that town was attacked, and in many instances – Valognes, Tilly and Caen, for example, were almost entirely destroyed. Whilst the purpose of this book is to record and not moralise, it is impossible not to wonder, as one becomes familiar with the people, the towns and the countryside, whether it could not have been possible to simply bypass the areas of most resistance and thus make them irrelevant, still maintain a prudent watch, and get on with the advance.

As was confirmed in the Pacific War, the technique of island hopping, leapfrogging the more heavily defended enemy occupied territory, capturing the supply bases, or amputating the flow of supplies – isolating the strong points from replenishment, can be as effective as bombardment, and far less costly in terms of lives, damage, effort and ammunition. It may be an emotional opinion which military experts could demolish, but this possible option must pass through the mind of any thoughtful visitor in Normandy.

Some Norman cities or towns escaped, Bayeux was one, and some people even had time to celebrate. But for others, the invasion was the forerunner of many grim days.

Today, towns and villages show little evidence of wartime damage, although other traces of the war remain. The *Omaha Beach* breakout, then sandy and bare, is still identifiable, but covered now in grass. In Carentan, the severely damaged buildings around the square and the railway junction have been faithfully restored, and although now minus its clock, the magnificent Church of St Mary which dominates the hub of tiny Ste Marie du Mont, is as it was.

Montebourg and Valognes have long since been rebuilt, and substantial improvements have been made to the foreshore at Arromanches. Spindly-trunked trees which were becoming established in the church square at Ste Mere Eglise in 1944, today are solid, healthy specimens, the rubble at Crisbeq, now pasture and hedges.

Peaceful, rural Normandy, which for centuries had escaped war, found itself involved in a savage conflict not of its making, with each town and village involved. There were those which through their strategic positioning, or because they were in the path of the armies, became more involved than others. There were some which were fortunate not to have been in the front line, but became embroiled after the 6th of June as the tide of battle engulfed them.

Normandy will never be the same, however well the scars of war are covered. Daily life within towns containing relics and museums, re-named towns, squares and streets, with the tourists, provides a constant reminder of more than 1,450 days of German occupation and the period of violence and peril which followed.

THE TOWNS

Notes for the Tourist

The main towns involved in D-Day and some of those impacted by the Battle of Normandy are grouped in the three Departements (Manche, Calvados and Seine Maritime), running from *Utah* in the west to *Sword* to the east. Museums and cemeteries are also listed.

MANCHE

Audouville-la-Hubert

On the D14, directly behind Utah beach, 2.5 miles (4 km) from Ste Marie du Mont. The Leconte farm, once owned by the Cotelles, was the site of the first US command post in France.

Avranches

Near Mont St Michel, Avranches is the point of the Patton breakthrough (Place Patton is American territory, with trees and earth imported from the United States), where the 4th and 6th US Armoured Divisions on the 30th of July, entered the town. On the day after, they captured Portaubault and its undamaged bridge over the Selune, to open up an entry into France from the west coast.

Avranches was the pivot for the breakout from Normandy, with Patton's troops spreading into Maine and Brittany, pushing the defenders in a loose semicircle from St Nazaire to Argentan and eventually into the Falaise pocket.

Linked with Mortain in a German counter attack on the 7th of August, in which four panzer divisions commanded by General von Lüttwitz, attempted to close the narrow gap. Close to success, this operation was beaten back by Thunderbolt and Typhoon aircraft, against which the German armour was almost defenceless, and the narrow slot remained open.

There is a 1944 museum nearby at Val St Pere.

Azeville (Battery)

On the seaward side of the village are the bunkers which once housed the 4-122 mm guns[1] of the 945th Army Coastal Artillery Regiment Commanded by Lt Kattnig. As the coast was not visible from the gunnery positions, a fire control bunker was established near the battery of St Marcouf (Crisbeq), a short distance away. Under a fierce flamethrower assault, and having exhausted all ammunition, the emplacement surrendered on 9th of June, saving more than 150 lives.

Barneville-Carteret

Small coastal port in unspoilt countryside featuring large sand dunes and stretches of deserted beach. On 18th of June 1944, the United States 7th Corps, approaching from the east, cut across the north-south highway, striking north towards Cherbourg. This caused some inconvenience for the German 77th Infantry Division which at the time was attempting to withdraw.

Brommy

Site of a heavy coastal battery which, on 25th of June, with two other batteries, engaged a squadron of Allied warships, succeeding in scoring hits on USS *Texas*, USS *Brien*, USS *Laffey* and HMS *Glasgow*.

Carentan and area

This town of less than 10,000 people is on the main railway line from Cherbourg to Paris, and with Ste Mere Eglise and Valognes, straddles the main N13 highway.

Landings by the US 101st and 82nd Airborne defended by the German 709th Division between Carentan and Valognes, both sides of the Merderet river.

---

1 Also recorded as 4-105 mm..

Identified from documents found by the Germans in a wrecked boat as being a primary Allied objective, the town was bitterly defended, and, originally expected to be a D-Day linkup between *Utah* and *Omaha*, was not captured until the evening, five days later. A counter attack next morning by the 17th SS Panzer Grenadier Division succeeded in gaining ground to the railway station, but eventually failed. With this came an end to the immediate threat to Ste Mere Eglise, and established Allied command of the N13 necessary for their thrust towards Cherbourg.

Occasionally, claims are made that Carentan was the first Norman town to be liberated, but at least Ste Mere Eglise, Ste Marie du Mont, and a number of other towns, villages and hamlets were freed beforehand.

Cemeteries
Huisnes sur Mer (Ger.) near Mont.
St Michel. Graves from the July engagements in the Battle of Normandy.
Marigny (Ger.) near St Lo.
Saint James, (US), between Avranches and Forgeres,
Valognes-Orglandes (Ger.)

Cherbourg (Also Gonneville, Osteck/Maupertus/Bretteville, Westeck)

A major port for cross channel ferries, Cherbourg was originally destined for greater things, but delays in implementing the objectives of the military planner Vauban, 300 years ago, delayed its opening until 1853. The inadequacy of the original port to handle trans-Atlantic liners until 80 years later, permitted other ports to gain prominence. From that point onwards, the significance of Cherbourg as a major port, diminished.

The city of approximately 90,000 people does not usually attract complimentary comment from travel writers, which is perhaps slightly unjust. The wharf area near the bridge is worth a stroll and there are some delightful and reasonably priced cafes in the area on the harbour frontage.

Walk to the left and then left again inland from the cafes, and there are a number of refurbished lanes with shops trading in a variety of articles from antiques to food.

From 12th of June, Cherbourg had been under threat, as Allied forces pushed up the N13, but it was not until 2 pm on the the 26th after suffering heavy casualties, with most of the massive fortifications surrounded, damaged, and out of ammunition, with scores of wounded expiring in the foul bunker air, that the German commander General Karl von Schlieben surrendered. Other pockets of resistance continued, mostly at the harbour front, where the dock and its historic tower had been blasted into the harbour basin, but this activity ceased on the 27th.

To the east, the Osteck network of forts near the airfield held out until 1.30 pm on the 28th of June. It was then that Major Küppers, visited by US officers and shown a map complete in all detail, and told what would befall them tomorrow when the navy and air force were called in, surrendered.

PLUTO fuel pipeline connected Cherbourg with Isle of Wight, 12th of August, 1944.

War and Liberation museum in Fort du Roule, on the opposite side of the basin, to the south-east.

Coutances

A delightful historic town, which influenced French history as far back as the 11th century. Centrepiece is the Cathedrale du Notre Dame. On high ground near the western coast of the Peninsula, the US 7th and 8th Corps headed for Coutances in their drive from St Lo towards Avranches in late July.

Crisbeq

A small hamlet neat St Marcouf, above which the batteries

commanding *Utah Beach* were sited. Listed in more detail under St Marcouf.

Douvres/River

As with the Dives to the east, the Douvres had flooded the surrounding countryside, its normal flow into the sea being impeded with sandbags and concrete barriers placed at the mouths of the river and its tributaries. The result was inundation of the low lying land, and death for many of the paratroopers who were discharged away from their assigned drop zones. Best estimates of losses through troops drowning, or equipment plunging below the water surface, was one-third troops and two-thirds equipment.

Dunes de Varreville

A strongpoint on *Utah Beach* prior to the D-Day landing, but demolished by well executed air raids and found abandoned by paratroopers (Lt Col Robert Cole US 502nd Regiment), when they reached the coast in the link up with Brigadier General Theodore Roosevelt's incoming assault troops. On the sparsely populated coastal road west of the *Utah Beach* museum (La Madeleine), a memorial to General Leclerc's 2nd French Armoured Division is prominent in a cleared area.

Foucarville

On the crossroads of the D14, 2.5 miles from the beach at Utah. Scene of the first recorded engagement of the 101st Airborne on D-Day. A platoon of twelve, under Capt Fitzgerald, attempted to capture the village, but was beaten back.

Gonneville (Cherbourg)

On the approach to Cherbourg, near the airport, a strongpoint which was part of the substantial chain of defences circling the city. The position was fiercely defended by young men of the German Labour Service, who, with ammunition exhausted, attempted to fight with their shovels. Not to be confused with the Gonneville near Merville, where Lt Col Otway and his 9th Parachute Battalion landed for their assault on the Merville battery.

Granville

An old fishing port, sold to England in the 15th century, now a terminal for Channel Island ferries. Granville, on its rocky headland, was in the path of Patton's strike to Avranches.

Hiesville

Glider landing field for US 101st Airborne, 4 miles from Ste Mere Eglise. One of the few completely accurate airborne landings, with most of the gliders landing on target. Although the majority were damaged by obstacles planted in the fields, the casualty level was surprisingly low, considering the practice was to load heavy machinery at the rear, where in a sudden stop, it would hurtle forward to crush the passengers in front.

Iles St Marcouf

Often shrouded by sea mist, but in clear conditions visible from the curving roadway slightly west of, and above St Marcouf, or from the shore, these rock islands off *Utah Beach* although unoccupied on D-Day, were heavily mined and booby trapped. Engineers attempting to clear the islands of non-existent guns were caught in this net and suffered heavy casualties for no gain. Another example of loss of life when it was preferable to bypass and leave well alone.

La Madeleine

Behind the dunes at *Utah*, and site of *Strongpoint W5*. The rivers Douve and Vire empty into the sea nearby. The many streams which also flow in the area were blocked at their mouths causing a deliberate flooding of the low lying land behind, resulting in many casualties through drowning as paratroopers fell into the inundated areas.

Accurate bombing virtually wiped out Lt Arthur Jahnke's defence network and cut off communication with the battery at the rear.

Today, part of the emplacement houses the Utah Beach Museum.

Lessay

A line drawn from Carentan to Lessay, chokes off the entire Peninsula at its southern point, so the town was a strategic goal for the Allies. The line was eventually established by the US 7th and 8th Corps driving south.

Maupertus (Osteck). See also Cherbourg

Now the site of a modern country airport ferrying passengers to inland France, the Channel Islands and Britain.

Merderet River

The flooded area was a disaster for the American paratroopers who landed in the water, or fell into flooded ditches. Dragged down by weight of equipment, some did not even surface, whilst those that did, desperately attempted to shed their loads, but most drowned.

Mesieres

A hamlet between *Utah Beach* and Ste Mere Eglise, Mesieres housed the crews of the battery at St Martin de Varreville, and was captured after a disproportionate loss of life on both sides.

Montebourg

Off the N14, between Ste Mere Eglise and Valognes, the town formed the western end of the German front line linking with the coast at Quineville. With Ste Mere Eglise occupied by the Allies, Montebourg was the first defence point, and orders were that it had to be held at all costs.

For twelve days the line held, then facing a two-sided attack from American armour, and using their last supplies of ammunition, the defenders withdrew under cover of rain and darkness. The severely damaged town was rebuilt in the same stone.

Mortain (See also Avranches)

Occupied by US Lt Gen Hodge's 7th Corps, then caught in the 7th of August German counter attack, (O*peration Lüttich*), Mortain was so severely damaged as to require rebuilding. Montgomery's 2nd Canadian Corps were sent in to open up a corridor to Avranches, intending to join Patton's armour and curve around to Falaise.

Relentlessly pounded from the air by waves of more than 1,100 flying fortresses which deliberately cratered the land and blocked town streets with rubble to impede progress and manouvering of the panzers, shelled by both sides and caught in the centre of the battle, the town crumbled.

Today, Mortain is known for spectacular waterfalls, leafy, shaded woodlands and its Abbey.

Museums

Cherbourg. Liberation Museum at Fort du Roule.
Utah Beach Museum. At strongpoint W5. La Madeleine.
Ste Marie du Mont. Small unique museum compiled by locals.
Ste Mere Eglise. US Airborne Museum.
Avranches. Breakthrough Museum.

Periers (West of St Lô)

Between Lessay and St Lô. Subjected to the dropping of advanced detonation bombs which minimised cratering but were particularly effective on troops and houses. Assaulted by the 8th US Corps on 25th of July, en route to Marigny.

Pont l'Abbe (See also Merderet)

Between the Merderet and the Douve on the edge of the Marais de la Sensuriere. Heavily inundated swamps which claimed the lives of many American paratroopers who jumped from their aircraft too early.

Quineville

Seafront hamlet which formed the eastern limit of the German lines to Montebourg. The line held for twelve days, but being on the coast where Allied attack was almost unopposed, Quineville folded before the remainder of the line.

St Lô

Vital pivot point of the US offensive. Intersection of the main D900, D972, D999, N174, D6 highways and many smaller roads, control of St Lô was important. Consequently, fighting was fierce and the town was reduced to rubble. Originally planned to be taken within 10 days of landing, St Lô was not captured until 32 days after that originally scheduled.

St Marcouf (Crisbeq)

On the rises above *Utah*, ten minutes' drive from Ste Mere Eglise, and well back from the coast, the battery of St Marcouf commands the picturesque countryside. Today's peace contrasts with the hell of high explosive and shattering concrete which began on the 6th of June, and continued for many days afterwards. For reasons of safety, the connecting trenches, open until 1991, have been filled in. The story of St Marcouf is described at the conclusion of Part 4.

Ste Marie du Mont

Behind *Utah Beach*. Once the beachhead had been established, troops filed inland to join paratroopers moving seaward. In their path was Ste Marie du Mont, and in the centre of the road, in the main square, the 12th to 14th century church of St Mary from which US scouts signalled the all clear to their comrades. The town was not much damaged in the landings, and contains a small unique museum commemorating Danish sailors who participated in D-Day. In summer, trees which surround the church provide welcome lunchtime picnic shade, and there is a delightful small bistro on the corner of the square.

St Martin de Varreville

Also behind *Utah Beach*, housed the support battery for *Strongpoint W5*. Because of communication problems, the battery of 122 mm guns (1261 Artillery regiment) did not fire on the beach. One otherwise reliable account notes that the guns were not fitted. They were.

Ste Mere Eglise

The town of the paratroopers, and today, very much the hub of tourism in the US sector.

Mayor Alexandre Renard's first-hand account of the occupation of Ste Mere Eglise, the town's liberation, and the cost of that freedom, is obtainable from the town's main book store.

About thirty paratroopers of the 82nd Airborne were blown into the town in the early hours of D-Day, many of them being killed on landing. In a disastrous panic move which caused the route north to be partially opened to the Allies, the occupying German flak unit withdrew prematurely soon afterwards, and US paratroopers quietly occupied the town before daylight.

There were a number of counter attacks, and for many days Ste Mere Eglise was shelled by the battery of Azeville and mobile artillery in an attempt to re-take the town. Although Azeville was captured, and forces to the south and west driven back, it was not until the 13th of June, with the arrival of tank reinforcements at Carentan, that the danger from enemy armour coming from the east was eliminated.

The Airborne museum situated alongside the church square is of exceptional standard. Good small bistros in the town, the bar and restaurant of Motel John Steele should not be missed, and neither should the Thursday market in the church square.

St Saveur le Vicomte
SW of Valognes. The old fortress was damaged in 1944 during the thrust of the 9th US Division from Ste Mere Eglise through Pont l'Abbe to Barneville and Portbail.

Utah Beach – (East of Quineville to La Madeleine)
Instead of landing at Dunes de Varreville as intended, actual touch-down was La Madeleine, about one mile south of target. The defence, *Strongpoint W5*, had been wrecked by accurate bombing, and shelling from long and close range, and the defenders, including their commander, captured.

(See also La Madeleine, Museums.)

Valognes
With Montebourg, in the path of the US advance on Cherbourg, and tenaciously defended by the Germans, being almost totally destroyed in the period 7th to 18th of June. Rebuilt in concrete. Cider museum open in Summer. Vitrified stoneware pottery still produced by medieval wood firing processes is on display and for sale.

Westeck (Cherbourg)
With Osteck, perimeter defence for Cherbourg, and in June 1944, was newly completed. Manned by the remnants of a number of diverse units,

including Luftwaffe air and ground personnel, older naval ratings, clerks, labourers and conscripted civilians. Vulnerable to attack from the land, the forts still held out for two days after the defences within Cherbourg collapsed.

CALVADOS

Arromanches les Bains

Important part of *Gold Beach*, now the centre of tourism for the British/Canadian sector.

The *Mulberry* caissons can be seen from the town foreshore, and good views obtained from the road above Arromanches coming in from Port en Bessin, and from the cliff on the other side of the town on the Ouistreham road. Can become very crowded with tourists.

Arromanches was liberated from the rear, the Allies coming in from Le Hamel in the late afternoon of 6th of June, but not completely securing the town until next morning.

Excellent museum (6th of June Exhibition) on the right hand side of the foreshore carpark.

Asnelles (see Le Hamel)

Bayeux

Home of the famous tapestry, Bayeux was only slightly damaged in the invasion, being liberated on 7th of June by the British 50th Northumbrian Division which had landed at *Sword*.

Although other French towns had been secured well before it became Bayeux's turn, Bayeux can claim to be the first French city to be liberated. Some British patrols had entered the town on the evening of the 6th but it was not until the 8th that the last of the German defenders retreated.

On 9th of June an attempt to regain Bayeux was launched by Panzer Lehr 2nd Battallion which came within three miles, but was pulled back for the defence of Tilly.

Memorial museum to the Battle of Normandy on the western side of the city.

Bernieres sur Mer
Juno Beach, the Canadian objective. Offshore reefs were a problem as they did not have sufficient water covering them at low tide, and it was necessary to run in as the tide covered the rocks – the same tide which was covering the mined obstacles in the shallows. The perfect example of *Catch 22*.

Bernieres
Part of an extended east-west German line established on 10th of June for the defence of Tilly. From Bernieres to Torteval and Anctoville, it ran east to Verrieres (north-west of Tilly), and Cristot, north-east of the town.

Benouville
On the Caen Canal, famous for the copybook assault by Major John Howard's glider borne Oxford and Buckinghamshire Light Infantry. The canal bridge was subsequently named *Pegasus Bridge*. The first home on the left, coming off the western side of the bridge, is thought to be the first French house to be liberated.

Bretteville – (North-west of Caen)
Scene of a bitter fight between the 25th Panzer Grenadier Regiment, the 12th SS Panzer Regiment, and the 7th Canadian Brigade. Was captured from the Canadians, but without infantry to support their drive, the tanks were forced to abandon the town.

Bretteville – (South of Caen)

Featured in Montgomery's 7th of August *Operation Totalise*, an all-out assault by armour and air on the German lines south of Caen, with the objective of breaking out into the area of Falaise, then wheel west to attack from the rear, German armour heading for Avranches.

Breville

Glider landing area near Benouville and Ranville, close to the Orne which was the scene of the first D-Day landings. Not to be confused with Breville sur Mer, which is near Granville on the West coast, and in the path of General Patton's 3rd Army during the Battle of Normandy.

Cabourg and Dives sur Mer

On the coast between Merville and Houlgate, Cabourg is near the mouth of the Dives, the river which claimed the lives of many paratroopers before they had even fired a shot. Being to the east of the Caen Canal, the towns were undamaged during the landing operation, although the Merville battery was less than 4 miles (6 km) away, and the centre of a generally inaccurate air attack, paratroop landings, and a subsequent naval bombardment.

Caen

Scheduled for capture on 7th of June, Caen was possibly the largest lost opportunity of D-Day. Sparsely defended, the British could have entered the city, but held back, and the Germans were handed the opportunity to consolidate and defend, a defence which would take the Allies ten weeks to overcome.

Beginning in mid-April with a devastating raid, from early May Caen was relentlessly bombed, being the target for more than 10,000 tons of explosive, in addition to being heavily shelled from sea and land, the combined effect being destruction of three quarters of the city. In total,

Caen experienced fractionally more than 1,000 air raids during the war, the final raids occurring on July 8th and 9th.

On D-Day, raids began shortly after 6.30 am, pinpointing selected areas such as the railway station and troop emplacements, but spilling out into residential and commercial areas with heavy loss of civilian life. Some of the popuation took refuge in buildings which were identified and not attacked by the Allies, and many lived underground for weeks in the Fleury quarries, on the city's southern boundary, until the savage battle ceased.

It was not until the 22nd of June that the Allied attack on Caen began in earnest, with a heavy artillery barrage across the Odon river as a prelude to capture of *Hill 112*. The hill was a strategically important piece of land to the south-west of the city, around which the battle would rage for the next four weeks. On 12th of July *Operation Jupiter* was launched by Sherman tanks of the 4th Army Brigade and the 43rd British Infantry Division, which suffered more than 7,000 casualties. Battle casualties included 22,200 British troops and airmen, and 3,000 civilians.

Caen Canal

The artery running 9 miles, (15 km) between the port of Caen, and the mouth of the Orne at Ouistreham. The first glider and parachute landings occurred in the area of Ranville and Benouville, the bridge over the canal (now named *Pegasus Bridge*), was the first D-Day objective captured, and held until the arrival of Lord Lovat's 1st Special Service Brigade.

Carpiquet

The busy airfield serving Caen, close enough to the coast for aircraft movements to be observed through the periscope of the midget submarine waiting offshore to mark one boundary of the British/Canadian sector. Objective of the Canadian 9th Brigade and 27th Tank Regiment, which was severely shot up by the German 2nd Battalion of panzer grenadiers. The panzer regiment under the command of Brigadeführer Kurt Meyer, caught and virtually wiped out the Canadians as, with their flanks unprotected, they rushed towards the Caen Bayeux road.

Cemeteries
Omaha:
Colleville Saint Laurent (US).

Inland from Omaha:
La Cambe (Ger.). On left hand side of N13 heading west.
Marigny-la-Chapelle (Ger.)

Gold Beach:
Banneville la Campagne, near Caen
Bayeux
Brouay
Chouain
Fontenay
Ryes
St Manvieu
Sequeville
Tilly

Juno Beach:
Le Beny Bocage
Beny sur Mer (near Courselles), (Can.)
Cambes en Plaine (UK)
Lisieux

Sword Beach:
Banneville
Bretteville-sur-Laize
Douvres
Fontenay-le-Pesnel

Grainville (Polish)

Hottot-les-Bagues

Hermanville sur Mer

Ranville

Chateau Haut

Inland from *Utah* and on the edge of the territory covered by the paratroopers of General Gavin's 82nd Airborne. Headquarters of one of the "absent generals", Major General Falley of the German 91st Air Landing Division who was attending a war games exercise as the Allies parachuted in to his area.

Colleville Montgomery and Colleville Montgomery Plage

The first is a small town inland from *Sword Beach*, near which the German 716th Infantry Division, comprising many conscripted Poles, had installed comparatively strong fortifications of 105 mm guns in concrete casemates, and a number of concealed but unprotected field guns. The defenders surrendered to the 1st Suffolks without a fight.

On the beachfront itself is Colleville Montgomery Plage. Sited between Lion-sur-Mer and Riva Bella, the defences of this narrow strip of beach provided what was probably the stiffest resistance of the *Sword* sector, with the 2nd Yorkshires losing more than 200 men within minutes of landing.

Their troubles were made worse by a heavy artillery bombardment of the beach, which, similar to the *Utah* and *Omaha* sectors, was assisted by ranging in on the barrage balloons used to deter the almost non-existent Luftwaffe. The reason was identified, and the balloons cast adrift.

Colleville sur Mer

With Vierville, the nearest village to *Omaha Beach* and site of the impressive United States' cemetery, where 170 acres (70 ha) of French soil gifted to the United States by the French Government contains 9,385 graves. The remains of many servicemen have been transferred to their home towns at the request of relatives.

The tragedy of *Omaha* was brought upon by two principal events; the landing craft being forced off course by wind and tide, and the almost useless pre-landing air assault, when, bombing by stopwatch through the heavy cloud cover, all 13,000 blockbuster bombs dropped by 330 B-24 bombers exploded wide of their marks. The US 8th Air Force command, acting on the side of caution in case the bombs landed amongst their own arriving troops, held the bomb drop off for a few seconds, and completely missed the four mile stretch of target.

Close as it was to the landing, the town was not liberated until 10 am on the 7th of June, when the last of the defenders was driven from the severely damaged church.

Commes

Inland from Port en Bessin, Commes was circled by the 47 Royal Marine Commando in their drive for the Port. The town now houses the best naval artifact museum in Normandy, containing a wide range of D-Day relics recovered from the sea bed by Jacques Lemonchois. Well worth visiting, as there are few reminders on the beaches.

Courseulles

A small town of barely 3,000 people, well known for its succulent oysters, with an oyster museum sited on the road to Arromanches. Courseulles was the centre of *Juno Beach*, and site of the landing of the Canadian Regina Rifles (7th Brigade). Here, the defences were virtually unharmed and mounted a stiff resistance against the invaders.

The western marker submarine *X20* submerged offshore on 4th June.

At least 32 separate emplacements housing weapons ranging from machine guns to heavier artillery and mortars poured fire down on the Canadians who suffered heavy casualties. The town had to be cleared house by house, street by street, and some captured ground recovered again as the defenders moved back into the cleared areas through tunnels. Courseulles was in Canadian hands by 10 am.

A good example of the Duplex Drive Sherman tank, recovered from the sea in 1971, is in the main square, and the market on Fridays is excellent.

Cresserons

Place du 22nd Dragoons, commemorates the British mine clearing (flail) tanks.

Dives Valley/River

The Dives claimed as many lives in the early hours of D-Day, as did the enemy. Not to be confused with the Douve, which also extracted its toll of the American 82nd Airborne, the Dives and its valley drowned countless paratroopers before they even sighted their objectives. The toll can be accurately termed "countless", because nobody knows exactly how many lives were wasted, as many paratroopers sank without trace.

The marshes were criss-crossed with ditches 7 feet, (2 metres) deep, and the entire complex was flooded by blocking off the exits of the river and streams. Of the D-Day deaths, it is relevant to mention that drowning in swamps, rivers and the sea, and not enemy action, was probably the principal cause of death. But we will never know, as the sea claimed the weighted bodies, as did the swamps and rivers.

Falaise

Not a D-Day objective, but as the last stand of the German army in Normandy, must be included, Falaise, a peaceful little town was severely mauled in the final action of the Battle of Normandy. The *Falaise Pocket*, a 22 by 11 mile (35 by 18 km) wide trap in which the German 7th Army and 5th Panzer Army were confined, was the result of a relentless push from the Allies, with the US 15th Corps to the south, the 12th British Corps to the west, Canadians and Poles closing in from the north.

The Argentan-Falaise-Chambois area contained more than 100,000 men of the German army, and after a battle lasting a week in which Allied fighter-bombers and artillery swept the ground with shells, rockets and bombs, 40,000 were captured on the 25th of August, the remainder being killed, and a few escaping.

Fontenay (near Tilly)

Fontenay is typical of a very confusing system of naming towns in which there can probably be more than one of the same name, so it is usually advisable to check alternatives before concluding that the town is in fact the one you expect it to be. There are at least two other Fontenays – Fontenay sur Mer, about 55 miles (90 km) away in neighbouring Manche, and a Fontenay well to the south in Lower Burgundy. Fontenay, near Tilly was the scene of a panzer v artillery battle in which the 2nd Battalion Panzer Lehr under the command of Prince Schoenburg-Waldenburg and British-Canadian anti-tank artillery fought in orchards. With the panzers defeated, the Allied forces turned towards Tilly, to begin the first phase of the capture and virtual destruction of that town.

Gold Beach (Port en Bessin to La Riviere)

This beach forms an umbrella over Bayeux, and it was Bayeux which was perhaps the least damaged of all principal Norman towns or cities.

The British Northumbrian Division landed at 7.25 am at Ver sur Mer and Asnelles. Linked up on 12th of June at Carentan with US troops off *Omaha*. Port en Bessin was captured from the rear by the 47th Commando. At Longues sur Mer, the German long range battery was knocked out by *Ajax*, the French cruisers *Montcalm* and *Georges-Leygues*.

Tilly sur Seulles changed hands 23 times between the 7th and 25th of June.

Grandcamp-les-Bains (Grandcamp Maisy)

Although on the seafront, the town was not an initial D-Day objective. In fact, the French Resistance area commander, Jean Marion, thought they had been forgotten, particularly as the 47 mm seafront gun, positioned to range in on what was now *Utah Beach*, was firing away, unmolested. Marion had sent a message to London some days previously, alerting them to the existence of the emplacement, but later, as he watched, a Royal Navy destroyer approached from the gun's right hand side, the side to which it could not traverse, and methodically blew it up.

The memorial on the seafront of this small fishing port represents a Halifax bomber of the French 346 and 347 squadrons, RAF which participated in the softening up operations in the Maisy la Martiniere-Maisy la Peruque area, and the stretch of coastline leading up to Pointe du Hoc.

A small number of indoor-outdoor quayside cafes at which to pause during the day to admire the harbour basin and the fishing fleet's activities.

Graye Sur Mer

The centre of *Juno Beach* activity, near Courseulles, the town is site of the first breakout from *Juno*, and famous for the gentry which passed through shortly afterwards, including General Sir Bernard Montgomery, Winston Churchill, General de Gaulle, and King George the sixth who landed on the 16th of June from HMS *Arethusa*. An exhibit of an AVRE mortar tank is in the town, the mortar being a hollow bomb which was termed the "flying dustbin", having a short trajectory which covered less than 100 yards.

Hermanville

Town on *Sword Beach* which is packed with D-Day history. From here, Lord Lovat's commandos pushed inland to relieve Major Howard's paratroopers clinging to *Pegasus Bridge*. Much of the military water supply came from Hermanville, with multiple taps attached to the Mare Saint-Pierre well, and a plaque marks the spot. There is a British cemetery, and a number of other commemorative plaques in the town. Off Hermanville, the French warship *Courbet*, with other merchantmen forming the *Gooseberry* fleet, was scuttled to form part of the outer harbour.

Hottot

The left hand corner of the Tilly triangle with Fontenay, and scene of the post D-Day battle for *Hill 112* between Major General Fritz Bayerlin's Panzer Lehr and Montgomery's 2nd, 49th and 50th Armoured Divisions. From the 16th of June the battle raged, and Hottot changed hands a number of times. But with the Germans in possession on the 2nd of July, orders came from C in C West for the Panzer Division to withdraw to St Lô, and be replaced by a Luftwaffe field division inexperienced in infantry combat. This unit was soon defeated, and the highway to Caumont L'Evente opened.

Isigny s. Mer

In the path of the link-up between *Utah* and *Omaha Beaches*, Isigny was heavily damaged on the 8th of June by a combined artillery and air bombardment in which more than half this small estuary town was destroyed. Fortunately, the town was captured the following day with little additional damage being inflicted, and with the 18th century chateau and 13th century church still standing.

In common with many Normandy towns, Isigny also has a "Best in France" claim. Theirs is for cream and butter, with also a strong bid for the delicous *pré-salé* lamb grown on the salt marshes.

Juno Beach (Graye sur Mer to Luc sur Mer)

Canadian sector. Reefs on eastern half. Canadian 3rd Infantry Division landed Bernieres and Courselles, with town of St Aubin sur Mer providing stiff resistance. Bernieres fell at 8.30 am, Courseulles was captured by 10 am, but the Canadians would not be in St Aubin until the following day.

La Cambe

On the left hand side of the N13 heading West, is this large German military cemetery, established in 1948. With good parking alongside the highway, a visit restores some balance to the D-Day story, and is, with the *Omaha Beach* Cemetery, a sobering experience.

Langrune

This seaside town lies between St Aubin sur Mer and Lion sur Mer, directly in the path of a planned link up between 48 RM Commando and 41 RM Commando. The seafront was defended by a massive array of weapons surrounded by a 40 metre minefield, and the emplacements were linked with accommodation in nearby houses by a network of tunnels. The latter made clearance of the town difficult, and fierce house to house fighting lasted until late in the evening of the 7th of June.

La Riviere

Eastern boundary of *Gold Beach*. The pre-invasion softening up had demoralised the defenders and the town was captured at 9.30 am. This prepared the way for a swift thrust towards Bayeux and contributed significantly to the Allies' ability to capture Bayeux on the 7th of June, with minimal damage – the first French city to be liberated in the Normandy landings.

Lebisey

The Lebisey Ridge, (or Rise), a hill close to, and north of Caen, was the jumping off point for the 22nd Panzer Regiment in its 6th of June drive for the sea. Splitting the 3rd Canadian and British Divisions, its grenadiers reached the sea at 8 pm, but the tanks which were to follow ran into Canadian anti-tank units, lost 14 of their number, and were forced to retreat into the wooded Rise.

Le Hamel (also Asnelles)

Western marker submarine *X20*, (Lt Ken Hudspeth, RANVR), was reported to have submerged off the town, 20 miles from the eastern marker submarine, *X23*, (Lt George Honour RNVR)[2]. The German 352nd Infantry Division defending the town escaped the aerial and naval assault almost unscathed, and lead by a 88 mm and 50 mm gun firing from the protection of concrete casemates, provided tenacious opposition to the incoming forces. The 88 mm was destroyed by a self propelled 25 pounder gun of the Essex Yoemanry, one of 24 successfully landed on the beach to support the infantry.

This was the planned landing zone of Lt Col Phillips' 47 Commando which had the task of landing, circling around, and capturing Port en Bessin from the rear. Following the 1st Hampshires, the commandos' fourteen vessels came under sustained and accurate fire from the undamaged defences, and were forced to deviate east, where they ran into submerged obstacles, sustaining major losses of personnel and equipment.

The main street is divided into three sections, commemorating the 1st Devonshire, 1st Dorset, and 1st Hampshire battalions of the 231st Brigade.

Le Ruquet

On one of the tracks which wind amongst the bluffs and dunes behind

---

2 Original operational maps contradict this, and place *X20* off Courseulles on the *Juno Beach* boundary.

Omaha Beach, this small hamlet contained a 50 mm gun for defence of the valley.

Lion sur Mer

Landing in this area was threatened by the guns at Merville, prompting the early morning attack on the emplacement by Lt Col Otway's paratroopers. Seaward are the reefs which had to be avoided (Les Roches de Lion). Also close to the scene of the breakthrough to the coast by the 1st Battalion Panzer Grenadiers, and a fierce counter attack by the German 3rd Battalion, 736th Grenadiers, with 105 mm artillery which petered out at the 12th century church. Mortar post at the intersection of Boulevard Anatole France and Rue des Ecoles.

Lisieux

Once designated a cathedral city, this status was lost in the early 19th century. Home of Ste Therese. Canonised in 1925, and author of the book, *Story of a Soul*, she died in 1897 of tuberculosis, at the age of 24. *Les Buissonets*, once her home, is now a museum, with the Saint's personal belongings on display.

Intended as the station for 12th SS Panzer on transfer from Belgium in April, the panzers were diverted further inland to observe General von Geyr's requirement of maximum room between the Division and the sea (against Rommel's wishes). Eventually, the assembly area for 1st SS Armoured Corps to the puzzlement of all, as this unit should have been heading for Caen and the coast.

Scene of the retreat of Lt Col von der Heydte's 6th parachute regiment which successfully filtered through the American lines, 1,006 survivors of an original regiment of more than 4,000. At Lisieux, on the bridge, Allied fighter-bombers caught the remnants, and in the rocket and cannon attacks which followed, less than 60 men of the regiment escaped.

Longues sur Mer

A Kriegsmarine battery of 4-150 mm guns, supported by searchlights, flak emplacements and 20 mm cannon, was sited on a high cliff 300 metres inland, and elaborately served by an observation and command post on the edge of the cliff.

Heavily bombed in the days leading up to the invasion, completion of the command post was delayed, and on D-Day could not observe the sea, as the mounds of earth left in place to camouflage the structure had not been removed. In spite of this handicap, the battery delivered an accurate fire upon the invasion fleet, engaging HMS *Ajax*, in a duel which was joined by the French cruiser *Georges Leygues*. Eventually, three quarters of the battery was disabled, and the emplacement captured without opposition, on the 7th of June.

Luc sur Mer

One of the beaches from which sand was collected as early as 1941. Luc's defence emplacement at Le Petit Enfer, consisting of fortified villas, (now most likely the local camping reserve), delayed the advance of 46 RM Commando until the evening of the 7th of June.

This is the town near which the German 192nd Panzer troops reached the coast in a split between the beaches which had not yet linked up. Had not the supporting armour been intercepted near Lebisey, it is possible a firm wedge could have been driven between the two invading forces.

Whether this could have been sustained in the face of German Headquarters' indecision and contradictory orders, the absence of the generals, and lack of stronger armoured reinforcements, coupled with Allied air superiority, is doubtful. However it would have given the German army time to collect themselves and mount a stronger resistance to the subsequent drive inland.

Merville-Franceville

Battery defending *Sword Beach*. Situated 4 miles (6 km) from the coastal town of Cabourg, the heavily fortified Merville battery was attacked and captured by British commandos of the 6th Airborne in the early hours of the 6th of June. The town of Merville was one of two mistaken by the support bombers as being the target, and heavily bombed by more than 100 Lancasters prior to the assault. Not one bomb dropped on the battery, and to compound the problem, most of the assault group's personnel and equipment was spread so far that only a small contingent, lightly armed, and without signalling equipment, tackled the defences.

Today, the emplacement is a fairly nondescript collection of low concrete bunkers overgrown by grass and weeds, on which the local cows stand to ruminate and survey the countryside. One of the bunkers has been converted to a museum which is open during June, July and August and closed each day for two hours from 12.30 pm.

Museums

Omaha Beach:
Vierville. Omaha Exhibition

Gold Beach:
Arromanches. Invasion Museum
Bayeux. Memorial Museum of the Battle of Normandy
Tilly sur Seulles. Museum for the Battle for Tilly

Sword Beach:
Benouville. 6th Airborne Division Museum
Caen. Memorial for the Battle of Normandy. Covers 42 acres
Merville-Franceville. Merville Battery Museum
Ouistreham-Riva Bella. No 4 Commando, Plc. Alfred Thomas
Hermanville. Sword Beach Museum

Omaha – (Pointe du Hoc, Colleville sur Mer, Ste Honorine)

Includes Pointe du Hoc . . . 225 rangers climbed cliffs to capture this battery which threatened the main beach assault. 1st US Infantry Division landed at *Omaha* 6.30 am but off course. Pinned down, considerable loss of life. Destroyers came in close and shelled the beach. Armour confined to a narrow strip of shingle and could not move. From the seafront road between Vierville and Colleville, closer to Vierville, a gap in the sandhills now grassed and marked with telephone posts, marks the breakout road from Omaha.

The United States military cemetery, and the approach, is US territory gifted by France. The graves occupy 172 acres (70 ha). Although many of the soldiers' remains were returned to the United States, there are almost 9,400 graves in the cemetery. Allow more than an hour to fully appreciate this immensely moving memorial to the sacrifice of thousands of young men.

Ouistreham – Riva Bella

The Eastern perimeter of the invasion beaches, and boundary of Sword. *X23*, the eastern marker submarine, commanded by Lt George Honour (RNVR), submerged off the mouth of the Orne, and through his periscope Honour could view aircraft using Carpiquet airfield to the west of Caen.

Severely damaged during the invasion, and with buildings now indicating little of their difficult past, Ouistreham is a car ferry terminal and large port for yachts, with a lighthouse from which excellent views of the coastline may be obtained. If you look closely, there are still signs of the occupation – a villa built in to a bunker, for example, or the gun emplacement near the lighthouse (originally there were three), and the car ferry terminal is built on a series of bunkers. At Riva Bella, concrete pyramids constructed as tank obstacles run alongside the path to the beach.

The seaside attachment of Riva Bella was extensively damaged and has been almost entirely rebuilt. Today's casino is built on the site of the original, which was destroyed in 1942.

Pegasus Bridge

Inland from Ouistreham, until 17th April 1994 the external appearance of the bridge remained virtually identical to how it was in 1944, with minor alterations to railings being the exception. On that day in 1994, 49 years and 10 months after D-Day, the bridge was replaced. The story of this important D-Day objective is fully told in the text. On the western bank are two good bistros, one has good food, and open air eating, and the other, good souvenirs.

On the eastern bank of the canal are memorials marking the landing places of Major Howard's gliders. Nearby, facing the canal, is the main memorial commemorating capture of the bridge. First house to be liberated in France.

Periers (North of Caen)

Scene of the abortive attempt by 21st Panzer to counter the *Sword* landing. Outgunned by the optics and range of the British anti-tank artillery situated on high ground between Periers and Bieville, the tanks were forced to withdraw, with losses. Integral with the battle for Caen, the Bieville-Periers area was to be the scene of many desperate encounters until the end of June.

Picauville

Near the Douve, the Merderet and their marshes, Chateau Haut, Pont l' Abbe, Beuzeville and nearby towns. Centre of the misdirected landing of the 82nd Airborne, many of whom were rescued by residents and safely conducted towards their correct zones.

Pointe de la Percee

Site of a small 77 mm gun emplacement, captured on the 7th of June. Camping ground nearby.

Pointe du Hoc

Scaled by 2nd and 5th Rangers. Please see *Omaha* and text.

There is an extensive amount of damage still evident, and on D-Day it must have closely resembled the moon. The entire ground has been ploughed over by shells and bombs, with scarcely a metre left untouched. One marvels at the capacity for humans to survive and still provide substantial opposition to the Rangers climbing the cliffs. As a balance, one glance down the cliffs, and it seems astounding that the troops could land, scale the sheer sides whilst under fire, still reach the top within a short time, then capture the emplacement in fifteen minutes.

Port en Bessin

Delightful fishing port, the boundary of *Omaha* and *Gold Beaches*. The fort is one of Vauban's (his work is also evident at Cherbourg), and there are odd relics of the German occupation, including one of their forts near Vauban's.

An attempt to take the port from the sea would have been difficult, as the harbour basin entrance is narrow and tidal. Following the decision to capture from behind, 47th RM Commando landed near Le Hamel, fought their way through, circled, coming in on the blind side of the defences shortly after a naval bombardment had ceased on the 7th of June. The commandos swarmed down along the quay, where now cafes serve an array of succulent seafood to tourists.

The port was delivery point for one of the PLUTO pipelines, the others being Cherbourg and Ste. Honorine. Port en Bessin's terminal was delivering fuel, oil and water on the 25th of June through a six inch pipe, the fuel coming in at a maximum rate of 8,000 tons a day.

Ranville

First landings of British Airborne 5th Parachute Brigade, Oxford and Buckinghamshire Regiment. Bridge over the Orne. Ranville taken by airborne unit of Lancashire Fusiliers. Major Howard's paratroopers took bridge over the Orne, (*Pegasus*), nearby. The fields near Ranville were soon littered with gliders which had discharged their cargoes to back up the initial airborne and seaborne troops.

Riva Bella
Please refer to Ouistreham, as Riva Bella adjoins on the seaward side.

Saint Aubin
Landing place of 88th Royal Marine Commando. Although they landed on time at 7.30 am, and were able to enter the town by midday, so fierce was the defence that it was not until the next day that St Aubin was in Allied hands.

Ste Honorine
Eastern boundary of *Omaha Beach*.

Bunker built into the cliffs near the town and battery in the cliffs more than 100 feet (30 m), above *Omaha*, commanded by Major Werner Pluskat. The Major, with his dog, Harras, featured in the film *The Longest Day*.

Saint Laurent Sur Mer
Site of the first United States airfield. In the elevated church cemetery, with headstones facing south, are the graves of three British commandos killed during a raid in September 1942. The objective of the raid was to bring back information, but of the nine man squad, eight were either killed or captured.

Sword Beach (Lion sur Mer to Ouistreham)
British and French commandos landed first, 4th Commando (Commandant Philippe Kiefer), 6th Commando (Lord Lovat), captured the strongpoints of Riva Bella, Colleville-Plage, Lion sur Mer. Followed

by infantry and armour of the 51st Highland Division who were last off the beach at Dunkirk. Objective was Caen. Beaches exposed to German long range guns at Le Havre. Please refer to the main text.

Tilly

Tilly sur Seulles. Part of the German, Cristot-Tilly-Verrieres-La Belle Alpine front line. The main force of the British offensive after D-Day was directed at Tilly, resulting in destruction of most of the town. Tilly was taken and re-taken 23 times between the 7th and 25th of June. Museum of the Battle for Tilly.

Troarn

Site of one of the bridges over the Dives marked for demolition early on D-Day, as it lay on the main road to Le Havre from which reinforcements could come if the highway was not breached. Destroyed by British sappers of Major Roseveare's unit.

Varaville

Scene of British paratroop landings in the early hours of D-Day.

Ver sur Mer

The small town was captured by the 7th Battalion, Green Howards, without opposition, and formed the bridgehead of *Gold Beach*.

Verrieres

With Tilly and two other towns, formed the German front line defended with armour.

Verson

Divisional headquarters of Lt Kurt Meyer's 2nd Panzer Division, defending the Allied drive towards the notorious *Hill 112*. The town was entered by the British 11th Armoured Division on 27th of June.

Vierville sur Mer

Please refer to *Omaha Beach*.

Villers-Bocage

On the main south-west artery from Caen to Vire, and scene of armoured battles, where an incident illustrating the vast superiority of the German 88 mm gun and the 52 ton PzKpfw Mark V1 Tiger tank occurred. One SS Obersturmführer Wittmann is reported to have destroyed an entire convoy of 25 mixed armoured vehicles, including Shermans, with his Tiger's 88. The soft and muddy fields confined movement of armour to roadways where tanks and trucks were easy prey for 88 mms concealed in the wooded countryside.

A covered market is a feature of the town, which is now known for its meat industry.

Vire

On a strategic intersection, was virtually destroyed during the post D-Day battles. Vire is set in a beautiful countryside with the Vire River running through valleys and forests. The old architecture of the 15th century church and part of a 12th century castle remains.

Vire (River)

Flows from the town of Vire, through St Lô, entering the sea on the boundary between *Utah* and *Omaha Beaches*.

SEINE MARITIME

Dieppe

The port through which the Allies learned, at considerable cost, that capture of channel ports as part of an invasion, was not an option. Home of scallop fishing, Dieppe provides more than half France's scallops, and early each morning there is a fish market selling a wide range of seafood.

The 17th century castle on the seafront is now a museum, and in front of the castle is Square du Canada, a memorial to the early explorers, but now also a memorial to the commandos who lost their lives during the 1942 raid. On the D75, which runs close to the sea, is the Musee de Guerre, and approximately 2 miles (3 km) to the west, housed on the site of a radar station, and on the right hand side of the road to Rouen, is the cemetery for those killed during the raid.

La Roche Guyon

Rommel's Headquarters were in the castle.

Le Havre

Second largest port in France, and now fully recovered from the destruction of the war.

The port was originally named Francispolis, after Francois I, who commissioned construction of the port in 1517 to replace the nearby ports of Honfleur and Harfleur which were silting up. However, it was renamed shortly afterwards as Le Havre (The Harbour).

CHAPTER SIX

PRINCIPAL STATISTICS

FOR D-DAY, THE 1,453RD DAY
OF GERMAN OCCUPATION

Approximate lengths of D-Day beaches (actual active areas)

	Miles	Km
Utah	9.25	15
Omaha	13	21
Gold	12	19
Juno	6.25	10
Sword	5.5	9
Totals:	**46**	**74**

Span of coastline (Distance, Quinneville to Ouistreham)

56 miles   90 km

Land operations

Troops landed on D-Day: 156,205
Casualties: 3,400 killed, 6,900 wounded
Paratroopers landed: British 3rd & 5th Para Brigades* 4,255
                       US 101st Airborne*   6,600
                       US 82nd Airborne *   7,000

* *Numbers vary according to the source of information, but these are believed to be the most accurate. The 101st's records indicate that initially 3,500 men were missing, which reduced to 1,240 a month later. Some returned from prison camps after the war, but how many perished in the swamps, rivers, inundated* *areas and the sea will probably be never accurately known. On D-Day, 182 were confirmed killed and 537 wounded.*

        Equipment landed: 15,000 vehicles
                                      1,500 tanks
                                      3,000 artillery pieces

Air operations

Aircraft available: Allied: 15,090. Includes 3,500 gliders, 80 air-sea rescue, 4,190 fighter-bombers, 4,370 bombers, 520 reconnaissance, 1,360 transport.

                          German: 319, including 100 fighters*

Sorties: Allied: 10,743
                German: Less than 100.*

Losses: Allied: 127, plus 63 damaged
               German: 39, with 21 damaged*

Bombs dropped: Allied: 11,912 tons.

* *There is considerable difference between figures relating to German aircraft and results, with Allied records indicating a far lower level of availability and activity. Some indicate only three aircraft available in the Normandy area, and two sorties flown. This could be true, as the 124 aircraft of Lt Col Priller's Luftwaffe 26th fighter wing had been removed the previous day, leaving only two fighters in the immediate area. Using original data, the figures given relating to German aircraft are sourced from Luftwaffe records.*

Sea operations

Allied ships: 6,840, manned by 96,000 seamen. Includes 6 battleships, 23 cruisers, 122 destroyers, 5,000 transports plus frigates, sloops and landing craft.

Blockships (*Gooseberries*):   59
Caissons (*Mulberries*):   146, ranging from 1,700 tons to 6,044 tons
Losses: 2 destroyers, (USS *Corry* and *Svenner*), 291 landing craft

Totals, D-Day until the end of the Battle of Normandy, August the 25th.

US Troops landed:	1,200,000
British and Canadian troops landed:	800,000
German forces opposing:	732,000

Casualties

Allied:	206,700
German:	235,000 (and 208,000 PoW)
Civilian:	45,000

LINE OF COMMAND

```
                    SUPREME COMMANDER
                    General Dwight D Eisenhower
                    DEPUTY SUPREME COMMANDER
                    Air Chief Marshal Sir Arthur Tedder
```

AIR

AIR COMMANDER IN CHIEF
Air Chief Marshal
Trafford Leigh Mallory

- **9TH US AIR FORCE** — Lt. General Lewis Brereton
- **2ND. TACTICAL AIR FORCE** — Air Marshal Sir Arthur Coningham

ARMY

21ST ARMY GROUP
General
Sir Bernard Montgomery

- **1ST US ARMY** — Lt. General Omar Bradley
- **2ND. BRITISH ARMY** — Lt. General M. Dempsey

NAVAL

COMMANDER IN CHIEF
Admiral
Sir Bertram Ramsay

- **WESTERN TASK FORCE** — Rear Admiral Alan Kirk USN
- **EASTERN TASK FORCE** — Rear Admiral Sir Philip Vian RN

NOTES TO PHOTOGRAPHS

Few experiences can match that of re-visiting and retracing with your own footsteps, the scene of historic events, particularly when they occurred within a lifetime, half a century before. If it comes with photographs taken at that time, when each photograph can be compared with the subject today, the experience becomes unique.

The recent photographs reproduced in this book, represent but a small number of those taken during eight years of photography in Normandy, and have been selected to represent principal areas of the D-Day conflict.

The originals have been chosen from thousands held by the National Archives in Washington and the Imperial War Museum, London, and I both acknowledge and thank each organisation for their permission to spend many hours in their rooms and reproduce the work of war photographers in this publication.

Seeking the site of each photograph is in itself a challenge, and entering an unfamiliar town with a fistful of photos depicting the damaged buildings and rubble strewn streets of fifty years ago is in itself a daunting task. But gradually the options are narrowed down, street by street, until a chimney, attic, or vaguely familiar roofline stirs a faint recognition, and after a minute or so of photo shuffling, the matching photograph is identified.

For visitors wishing to undertake comparative photography, identification of even severely damaged areas can be made by critical examination of window groupings, chimney positioning and design, groups of attic roofs, landmarks, or the number of storeys. When desperate, and knowing the routes taken by the troops, the route taken can be retraced, as had to be done with photographs appearing on page 99, and this usually brings its reward.

    Photo credits: 1944   Imperial War Museum (IWM)
                                 United States' National Archives (USNA)
               1986-1994   Al. Woods (AW)
                                 Author (A)
                                 Corporate Visual Services (CVS)

PAGE

51   Pegasus Bridge. Gliders of Major Howard's Infantry (IWM B5233)
      Cairns mark the approximate landing areas, 6th June 1993. (A)

Until 17th April 1994, the bridge remained substantially analtered, having survived for 49 years and 10 months after capture with only minor changes to the superstructure, and new railings. On that day it was replaced, so this is probably the last published photograph of the original bridge as it was on an anniversary of D-Day.

The new bridge will doubtless withstand the heavy volume of 50th Anniversary celebratory traffic better than the original, but to the people involved, "their" bridge cannot ever be replaced. It's just not the same, either for the residents of Benouville, the troops involved, or regular visitors.

From the position of the reeds which mark a marsh on the right hand side of the photograph, Major Howard and his men narrowly avoided an unplanned splashdown in the early hours of that morning.

The glider landing area is in a depression on the right at the eastern bank, as one comes off the bridge. Closer to the canal, and to the bridge is the D-Day landing memorial, scene of the service on 6th June each year.

NOTES TO PHOTOGRAPHS 159

52 A Bren carrier crosses the bridge, June 1944. (IWM B5234)
    Traffic after the memorial service, 6th June 1993. (A)

When planning comparative photography, the added dimension of introducing contrasting situations increases the significance of the comparison. Wartime and Peacetime activities are about as disparate as it is possible to be.

53 Utah Beach landings, 1944. (USNA 80-G-252624)
    June 1993. (A)

1 km west of *Strongpoint W5* which now houses the Utah Beach museum.

In the absence of landmarks, tracking down this house, which could have been anywhere on the 90 km (56 miles) of coastline, required a number of visits. It was the last untraced photograph on the last day of the 1993 research, and when it was obvious that the sand dune profile was either a stretch of Omaha or Utah, but more likely Utah, two hours of driving along the quiet roadway behind the dunes revealed a barely visible, isolated roof and chimneys. Approach from the shoreline indicated the redesigned roof, the distinctive verandah, then the unchanged gate.

54 Omaha Beach breakout, June 1944. (USNA SC-190382)
    June 1993. (AW)

Visible from the esplanade, there are also a number of small concrete emplacements on the hillside, almost hidden by undergrowth. To the left, and a short distance away is the villa owned by Michel Hardelay, scheduled by the Germans for demolition on 6th June, but one building the invasion actually saved.

55 The Hardelay villa, 6th June 1993. (A)

Lawyer, Michel Hardelay's seaside home was due for demolition on the 6th of June. Last of the unique villas which lined the esplanade, its companions had been destroyed for their materials which were used for fortification construction. Ironically, when other people lost their homes on the day, Hardelay's was spared by the invasion.

A section of Normandy beach, June 1992. (AW)

During the painful but necessary process of culling photographs, many were put aside, including some showing islolated beach wreckage, fortifications in the dunes, and even the remaining stumps of the mine topped poles which formed *Rommel's Asparagus*.

All have one feature which this photograph illustrates – long flat beaches which low tide exposes for hundreds of metres, beaches completely open to fields of fire which swept all in their path, through which the troops had to pass. This was why the pre-invasion softening up process was so vital, and why the Allied losses were high when landings occurred in areas where the defences had remained comparatively unmolested.

Landings occurred at the low tide illustrated.

56 Pointe du Hoc. (CVS)

Scene of one of the most heroic D-Day actions in which three Ranger companies under the command of Lt Col James Rudder approached the sixty foot cliffs which they were required to scale and capture the clifftop batteries. Although emplacements had been pulverised by a particularly effective air and sea attack, the defenders were able to re-group and resist the Americans as they climbed their ropes and ladders.

Emerging above the rim of the cliffs, Rangers encountered a deslolate wasteland which had been worked over many times. Installations smashed, with smoking, cratered and churned up landscape extending for as far as they could see, it was a scene of utter desolation. Although today the ground is grassed and well tended, it is still interspersed with wrecked gun emplacements, and the entire landscape is deeply pitted with hundreds of craters from which slabs of fractured concrete protrude – graphically conveying the inferno of that day, fifty years ago.

57   Going home. (USNA 190287)
     N13 Flyover, June 1993 (A)

Mme Audiee Digeon following her release from German detention, Ste Mere Eglise, 6th June 1944. Accompanying her and the GI porter is young Jacques Bizette, *fils du garagiste*, who today operates a fuel and vehicle servicing garage in the town.

Whilst most Norman towns and the countryside remain unchanged, pressures of today's transport requirements caused the re-routing of the main N13 Cherbourg-Paris road from the main street (page 60), to its new position, although trucks still roar through the town, usually in the early morning hours. The two chimneys visible under the flyover and information from residents assisted locating the scene. *Merci M. Eon.*

58   Crisbeq, and one of the 210mm naval guns, soon after capture, 11th June 1944. (USNA SC-190388)
     Crisbeq today. (A)

This particular emplacement was taken in almost pristine condition, and subsequent damage is thought to have been caused by either an accidental triggering of the ammunition supplies, or post invasion experiments with explosives.

The two photographs can be matched by examining remnants of camouflage markings on the casemate wall. These markings were achieved by trowelling long thin rolls of paper into the surface cement during finishing.

59   The battery at Crisbeq, close to the town of St Marcouf. (USNA SC-275904)

The hamlet of Crisbeq was completely in the firing line, literally under the muzzles of the guns. (AW)

A good example of fortification work, the battery commands the coastline, being far enough removed to avoid exposure to close range frontal assault from troops and armour.

In the 1944 photograph, ships of the invasion fleet can be seen dotted on the narrow strip of sea. Today, the battery's surrounds are well maintained, with the two main casemates on the left hand side of the road after the turnoff from St Marcouf and the fire control bunker for Azeville to the right, which forms an excellent viewing platform.

60 Ste Mere Eglise, June 1944. (USNA SC-190286)
    June 1993. (A)

At the intersection of the N13 highway (across the photograph) and the road to the sea.

There was minimal fighting in the town itself, so this damage was probably caused by either the Azeville Battery, or German artillery sited on the Beuzeville road.

The story of Ste Mere Eglise is graphically told in the book of the same name, by Mayor Alexandre Renard, and illustrates the suffering of the civilian population, repeated in many towns across the nation.

61 The Church by the Sea – Ste Mere Eglise, June 1993. (A)

The effigy of Private John Steele, of the 82nd Airborne's 505th, Regiment, is permanently on display, hanging from one of the corners of the roof. Always on this side, it moves from corner to corner each year, so this may not necessarily be the actual position from which he hung whilst the slaughter raged in the square below.

When the Americans quietly gathered in the town in the early hours of D-Day, the premature withdrawal of the occupying German flak unit opening the way for taking up residence without a fight, snipers remained in the bell tower and were removed the next morning.

For the residents of Ste Mere Eglise, many days of danger and misery were to follow, as the Germans conducted a sustained assault in an effort to recapture this strategic town.

Memorial to PFC W.F. McGowan, killed in action, 6th June 1944. (A)

From Rowe Road, signposted at the entrance to Utah Beach, inland along the Norman laneways, similar memorials sustain memories of young men from a foreign land who gave their lives thousands of miles from their homes. Apart from the roadways, main thoroughfares have been renamed – Rue Gen. Gavin, Rue Eisenhower, the town of Colleville Montgomery, and the beaches themselves, particularly Utah and Omaha have permanently relinquished their previous identification.

62   Farming mussels, La Madeleine, *Utah Beach*, 1993. (A)

With D-Day wreckage removed from the beaches, storms and moving sands occasionally uncover buried debris. A sunken breakwater is a rare but constant reminder.

Normandy is famous for shellfish, and mussel racks, submerged at high tide, line the low water line, as did *Rommel's Asparagus* and other underwater obstacles fifty years beforehand. Today, mussel farmers tend their racks at low tide, and tractors towing trailers piled with bagged *moules* are just about the only hazard one now encounters.

Terrain which disrupted the advance in June 1944. (CVS)

Eroded by centuries of traffic and water, Normandy laneways are often a metre below the level of the ground on each side. Armour was confined to these narrow arteries, or if attempting to cross, became jammed in the banks. Improvisation, by salvaging Rommel's railway iron triangles, welding them into scoops and fixing to the front of tanks, assisted in partly overcoming this problem.

95   Entering St Marcouf, June 1944. (USNA SC-189918-S)
The intersection now much tidier than in 1944, but still identifiable. (CVS)

These troops are entering from the direction of the Crisbeq battery, but as Crisbeq remained active well after St Marcouf had been captured, the actual advance into St Marcouf occurred from the opposite end of the town.

96   Watching the rear. (USNA SC-189929-S)
Laneway off the main road, beside the church at St Marcouf. (CVS)

In assembling wartime photographs it is evident that the photographers would loose off a number of shots by swivelling around on the same spot, or remaining well within one area. In the case of St Marcouf, there are photographs on the main road, at the top of the lane, middle of the lane, bottom of the lane, all taken within a short space of time using the same soldiers. This was a garrison town, the nearby battery fought fiercely for many days after D-Day, so despite the seemingly alert air of the troops, it is likely the previous occupiers were long gone.

97   Carentan, June 1944. (USNA SC-190400)
June 1993, the angel's wing survived the invasion, but not the aftermath. (A)

In the town square, and easily identifiable, except that with attention fully absorbed in parking my car on market day, the monument escaped initial notice. It was only after a long and fruitless search, that approaching from the other side, I discovered my car parked three metres away! Simple tasks can become complex.

NOTES TO PHOTOGRAPHS 165

98 A US tank crosses the Cherbourg-Paris railway line at Carentan at its intersection with the N13 highway, June 1944. (USNA SC-190413-S)
June 1993. (A)

This is an example of tracking an area through identifiable features such as the odd shape of a chimney, an attic, or gable window. Closer examination indicated that the original photograph had been taken near the N13 and the railway. The unusual power pole sealed the matter.

99 Entering Ste Marie du Mont from the main Utah Beach exit on the road from La Madeleine, *Strongpoint W5*. (USNA SC-190247)
Minor alterations to the frontage, June 1993. (A)

The cheerful atmosphere is probably the result of the very low enemy resistance encountered during the Utah landing, and the absence of defence in the town.

100 Troops off Utah entering Ste Marie du Mont around the square of The Church of St Mary, June 1944. (USNA SC 190231-S)
June 1993. (A)

Ste Marie du Mont is as it was; quiet and neat. To the top right of the photograph, on the corner of the road, is a delightful bistro.

101 Flotsam of war. (IWM B6318)
The esplanade today. (AW)

Beach at Arromanches following the worst storm for 40 years, which devastated the Mulberry harbours between 20th and 22nd of June.

102 Arromanches, 6th June 1993. (AW)

To the east of the town, on the road to Ouistreham, is a lookout area from which the sweep of the caissons can be seen. In the town itself, the caissons beached by the storms which occurred soon after D-Day, and wrecked the installations, can be inspected from close range.

103 Arromanches seafront, 1944 and 1993. (IWM B5708 and AW)
   The excellent museum is to the left of this photograph.

104 General Sir Bernard Montgomery at Port en Bessin, 10th June 1944. (IWM B5314)
   Port en Bessin, 1993. (A)

105 War and peace. Coming ashore, Port en Bessin, 1944 and 1993. (IWM B5393 and A)

106 German flak ship rests on the bottom of the basin, Port en Bessin, 10th June 1944. (IWM B 5395)
   Fishing boats at the same wharf, 10th June 1993. (A)
   The town was captured from landward, with Col Phillips' 47 RM Commando entering along the pier on this side of the channel, to the left of this photograph.

Cover: Extremities of the D-Day beaches.
   June 1944. (IWM B5290)
   6th June 1993. (A)
   Troops marching from the east over *Pegasus Bridge*, Benouville, near the eastern perimeter, behind *Sword Beach*
   Quineville, western perimeter, *Utah Beach*

ABBREVIATIONS

AA	Anti-Aircraft
AVRE	Armoured Vehicle Royal Engineers (Tank)
DD	Duplex Drive (Amphibious) tank
HDML	Harbour Defence Motor Launch
HMS	His Majesty's Ship
LCF	Landing craft – flak
LCT	Landing craft – tank
LCS	Landing craft – support
LCP	Landing craft – personnel
LS	Landing ship
LSA	Landing ship – assault
LSI	Landing ship – infantry
LST	Landing ship – tank
LBE	Landing barge – engineering
LCK	Landing craft – kitchen
MGB	Motor gun boat
MTB	Motor torpedo boat
ML	Motor launch
POW	Prisoner of war
RAF	Royal Air Force
RANVR	Royal Australian Naval Volunteer Reserve
RM	Royal Marine(s)
RN	Royal Navy
RNVR	Royal Naval Volunteer Reserve
RM	Royal Marine
Ste	Sainte
USAF	United States' Air Force
USN	United States' Navy
USS	United States' Ship